Agonies Of Enjoyment

The Autobiography

of

William Russell Raiford

Bloomington, IN   Milton Keynes, UK
authorHOUSE®

AuthorHouse™
1663 Liberty Drive, Suite 200
Bloomington, IN 47403
www.authorhouse.com
Phone: 1-800-839-8640

AuthorHouse™ *UK Ltd.*
500 Avebury Boulevard
Central Milton Keynes, MK9 2BE
www.authorhouse.co.uk
Phone: 08001974150

© *2007 William Russell Raiford. All rights reserved.*

No part of this book may be reproduced, stored in a retrieval system, or transmitted by any means without the written permission of the author.

First published by AuthorHouse 5/16/2007

ISBN: 978-1-4343-0273-1 (sc)
ISBN: 978-1-4343-0272-4 (hc)

Library of Congress Control Number: 2007901962

Printed in the United States of America
Bloomington, Indiana

This book is printed on acid-free paper.

Prologue

Writing an autobiography can be difficult, especially when a portion of one's life has been spent in the quiet, discreet and unheralded service to one's country. In order to protect the identity of certain individuals and their descendants, I have had to change names, dates and, in some instances, even places. Nevertheless, the life experiences I am about to relate are true. The people are real. Some of the situations are known to several people; some are known only to a few. I have omitted several instances that happened because of their delicate nature as it relates to the security of both individuals and countries. The first part of my life's story, up until about age thirty, is straightforward, the normal recollections of "a gentleman of the Old South." But the majority of my life, thus far, is still cloaked in, what I prefer to call, "service to others." My father had an expression which I liked. It was not original with him, but hearing him say it impressed me greatly. "It's amazing what you can get done, if you don't care who gets the credit."

Foreword

When one begins to tell a story, it is usually best to begin at the beginning. In the case of this particular undertaking, I believe that the reader will appreciate knowing the origin of the title of this work first and then will more readily understand why it has been chosen. "Agonies of enjoyment" was an expression I had heard early in my childhood, but it was not until I had traveled the world for over fifty years and had been exposed to several languages and their idioms and colloquialisms and experiences that I realized and appreciated the true meaning of this expression. The initial reaction of several friends was to label the term an oxymoron. I must admit that my first interpretation sided somewhat with that impression. But later in my life, I was able to experience the extremes of both pain and joy as reactions to the same stimuli, and thus came to realize that the speaker of this expression, heard in my earliest childhood days, was in reality a wise and seasoned participant in everyday Southern life. I, therefore, have chosen it as the title of this work, my autobiography.

On many Sundays, my family, and occasionally lots of friends, would gather at the dining table of my father's only aunt, affectionately known by everyone as "Aunt Annie." On each occasion, after the dinner had been completed and all but a few lingerers had left the table, those colored workers who had prepared and served the meal would gather at the large work table in the kitchen for their meal. On the occasion I remember so well, I overheard Aunt Annie ask one of the women, whose name was Saffronia, but who was called "Froanie",

"Froanie, are you enjoying your meal?"

"Yassum, Miss Annie," came the reply. "Ah'm jes suffrin' agonies of enjoyment."

Having just completed the same meal, I immediately knew the meaning of her comment: The food was so delicious, and if she continued to eat at her present pace, the agonies of over-eating would definitely ensue.

Agonies Of Enjoyment

My family came to Georgia in 1798 from North Carolina. Maurice Raiford, my great-great-grandfather, fought in the American War for Independence as a Lieutenant in the Fourth Regiment of the North Carolina Continental Line. That particular Regiment saw much action and participated in many battles of the Revolution, to include Monmouth, New Jersey; and Philadelphia and Germantown, Pennsylvania; and spent the winter at Valley Forge with General Washington. When the victory at Yorktown, Virginia, ended the War in October, 1781, most North Carolina participants were granted some acreage for their military service. Maurice, sometimes listed as "Morris" in the military records of North Carolina, was granted acreage in the western part of that State, land that is now situated in Eastern Tennessee. After traveling westward to view his new holdings, he returned to Raleigh, to exchange a part of his land grant for a "more suitable" piece of land in the "new" State of Georgia. Having been successful in this attempt, he moved his family in 1798 to Jefferson County, to the lower part of the County along Blackwater Swamp Creek. Louisville, the County seat of Jefferson County, was the capital of Georgia from 1794 until 1807.

Maurice's first marriage, in Johnston County, North Carolina, in 1780, was to a woman who's first name was Polly. Her last name is not now known. This union produced a son named Isaac Wesley. Maurice's second marriage, in 1785, also in North Carolina, was to Asenath Hodges, whose father, John, had been a Captain in the Fifth Regiment of the North Carolina Continental Line. Asenath, as found in the Biblical Book of Genesis, Chapter 41 and verse 45, was the name of the Egyptian wife of Joseph, the son of Jacob. This union was blest with eight children. Over the next twenty-five-plus years, Maurice acquired much land in Jefferson County, while, for some unknown reason, he retained some of his original land grant in the Western North Carolina (Eastern Tennessee) area.

In his will, dated 28 April 1824, Maurice leaves specific items of household goods to his children, and divides his land holdings in similar distributions. His wife, Asenath, is not mentioned in his will, so it is assumed that she had pre-deceased him. However, on a map of Jefferson County, found in the Court House in Louisville, dated 1815, there appear two small squares denoting houses, one designated "Raiford" and the other designated "Widow Raiford." It is not known whose widow this was. Maurice's will was probated on 1 November 1826. He was born about 1757 in North Carolina, so his lifetime of approximately sixty-seven years was about normal for a male in that period of American history. In his will, he also mentioned owning some land jointly with (General) Solomon Wood, a well known Revolutionary patriot whose home site in Jefferson County is currently commemorated by a marker in downtown Bartow. In the southeastern portion of Jefferson County, where Georgia

State Route 78 crosses the Ogeechee River, the current modern concrete structure replaced the previous wooden bridge, first known as Pierce's Bridge, in 1878; but renamed Raiford's Bridge, in 1934.

Maurice named his children in his will as follow: Isaac W., who had married Lucinda C. Bradford on 1 December 1822; Matthew, who was born in Jefferson County, Georgia, on 12 July 1789, and who died in Culloden, Georgia (no longer in existence), on 16 April 1849 without issue; Maurice, whose wife was named Patience, and who died in Harris County, Georgia, after 1833; Lexe, who was then unmarried; Pency, who had married Michael Watson in Jefferson County, Georgia, in 1819; Capel, who was born in Jefferson County, Georgia, on 3 May 1804, and who married Rebecca Ann Hunt in Sandersville, Georgia, on 21 October 1841; Asenath, who was then unmarried; Campbell, who later married Elizabeth Walker Bostick in 1838; and Barden C.M., a minor. In the tax rolls of Jefferson County for the year 1825, Kenneth, Campbell and Barden are listed as orphans of Maurice Raiford. However, no child named Kenneth appears in his will and may have been either a grandson or a ward.

My great-grandfather, Capel, whose name is the Welsh word for "chapel", was born in Jefferson County, Georgia, in 1804, and married Rebecca Ann Hunt in 1841. The Hunt family had settled in Sandersville, Georgia, in Washington County, adjacent to Jefferson County, after the Revolutionary War. Rebecca Ann's father, William, had also served in the Revolutionary War, as an enlisted man. In the 1850 Census of Georgia, Capel is listed as a resident of Butts County. In the 1860 Census of Georgia, he is listed as living in Thomas County. Thomas County, Georgia, was created in 1825 and Thomasville was made the

County seat in 1826. The exact date of Capel's and Rebecca Ann's arrival in Thomas County is uncertain, but it was after 1850 and before 1860.

Having been born and raised in South Georgia, I was exposed to the languages and customs of several ethnic groups. My father operated a grocery and market for over thirty years in Thomasville, a town of about eighteen thousand people. It was eighteen thousand in 1900 and it was eighteen thousand in 1948 when I left home for West Point. The local joke was that the population remained the same because every time a baby was born, someone had to leave town. The truth was that our town had little industry, and the local population could support the demands of that industry. The advantages of living in a small Southern town during the period from the Depression until after the Second World War, were the stability it afforded in everyday life and the opportunity to get to know almost all its inhabitants, some of whom spent a lot of their time "tending" to the business of others.

Upon arrival in Thomas County, my family acquired quite a bit of farmland and settled in a community in the eastern part of the county known as Boston. My paternal great-grandfather, Capel, was a Methodist minister, a circuit rider whose rounds included southwest Georgia and northern Florida. (The site of the Florida State Penitentiary, located at Raiford in Union County in northeastern Florida, was named for Hunter Warren Raiford, a cousin of my great-grandfather, who operated a sawmill in that vicinity and is alleged to have given the land to the State of Florida for the penitentiary.) Capel's name appears on the initial transfer of land for the local Boston Methodist Church; and he and his wife, Rebecca Ann, are buried behind that Church, which is next door to the Carnegie Library.

Boston, Georgia, has the distinction of probably being the smallest community in America with a Carnegie Library. The origin of that distinction, while unproven, has, by tradition in my family, to do with an event on a Sunday afternoon in the late summer of 1910. Aunt Annie's brother, Johnnie Sherrod, and his wife, Addie, lived on the main street of Boston, U.S. Highway 84. On one particular Sunday afternoon, while sitting in the swing on their front porch, enjoying a glass of iced tea, they observed a chauffeured touring car have a flat tire directly in front of their home. While Uncle Johnnie's colored help assisted the chauffeur in changing the tire, the passenger was invited to join them on the porch for a glass of tea. The passenger said that he was on his way to Florida and introduced himself as Andrew Carnegie, whose fame was unknown to my kin. After inquiring about the size of Boston and whether or not the city had a library; for the hospitality shown him that day, he stated that he would consider building a library for the city. Through the intercession of Mrs. O.T. Hopper, a Boston resident who was a friend of Uncle Johnnie and Aunt Addie, a letter was written to Mr. Carnegie, and the Library was built and stocked with a check for $6,000., which Mrs. Hopper received from Mr. Carnegie. This story has been a family tradition for many years. I can not attest to its validity, but having heard Uncle Johnnie relate it on several occasions, I believe it to be true.

Capel's son, Eugene Hodges Raiford, my grandfather, was born on 10 December 1860 in Boston, Georgia; and, on 16 January 1884, he married Alice Ida Credolia Sherrod, sister to Aunt Annie and her five brothers. After Alice's death, on 15 July 1891, Eugene married a second time into the McDonald family which had settled another community in the county, this one a few miles north of Boston, also on the eastern edge of Thomas County. Eugene's second wife was named Alice Wincey, whose grandparents were James and Serena McDonald. James McDonald appears in the 1840 Census of Thomas County, having come to Thomas County from Mecklenburg County, North Carolina. He was an Officer in the War Between the States and later a State Senator from this Georgia District. Originally called McDonald, the community's name was changed to Pavo in 1895 by the local Postmaster, a Mr. Peacock, who informed the Federal Government that there was confusion between the names of McDonald in Thomas County and McDonough up in Middle Georgia. (I doubt that many of the local residents were versed in the Latin language and knew that "pavo" is the Latin word for "peacock.") My grandfather, Eugene, left home in 1898, ostensibly to join the Army and to participate in the Spanish-American War. However, having searched the military records thoroughly, no citation for his service is found and no further information is known of his whereabouts.

My mother's family, the Shepherds, came to Thomas County in 1900 from a small, North Georgia community named Gillsville. Her ancestors were Scotch-Irish and migrated to Georgia from North Carolina in the Eighteenth Century, while my father's ancestors had come to Georgia by way of North Carolina from Virginia, to which they had emigrated from England in 1679. My mother's family were quite prolific; she had seventy-five first cousins, most of whom lived in or near Thomas County. My father had "only" sixty first cousins, but they too all lived in or around

Thomas County. I have often jokingly said that I am related to every fourth house in the County!

Believe it or not, the Thomas County (Georgia) Chamber of Commerce (TCCC) was formed in the Spring of 1540, shortly after the explorer, Hernando de Soto, arrived on the scene, at a site known as Anhayca. Of course, it was not then known as the TCCC; but the local inhabitants, mostly Cherokee Indians, knew the value of the land and its products and made good commercial use thereof. The local Indian Queen was a hard bargainer and a shrewd entrepreneuse who knew the attractiveness of the pearls which were to be found in the freshwater clams that inhabited the springs throughout the region. The pearls were rarely of uniform size and were rather small, but they had an iridescent quality that attracted de Soto and his men, who wanted them as souvenirs of the area to take back to their wives and girlfriends. This trade in pearls was quite lucrative and continued for several years, even after de Soto and his party had left for parts unknown. But the trading of pearls is almost unknown in Thomas County today, with the exceptions of a few local jewelers and occasionally a shrewd but unscrupulous party-goer.

I, William Russell Raiford, was born on a Wednesday morning, the 21st day of May, in 1930, at our residence, located at 107 East Mary Street in Valdosta, Georgia, the County seat of Lowndes County, some forty miles east of Thomasville. The time was recorded as 8:30. Checking the positions of the stars and planets for that date and time at that location, I am denominated a "Taurus on the cusp of Gemini." Astrologers will tell you that such a person is usually quite good with money management, but is also a very sensitive person associated with the arts. While I have devoted most of my life to managing the monetary affairs of others; and playing the piano and composing for piano, band, chorus and orchestra; I also enjoy the study and tasting of wines and good food. I have often said that I was born to be a guest!

My father, William Franklin Raiford, was born on 13 January 1889 in the family home on Simmons Road south of Pavo, Georgia. My mother was born on 19 May 1898 in Gillsville, Georgia. Before my father began his own grocery and market in Thomasville, he was associated with the Piggly-Wiggly Grocery Stores, one of the first self-service grocery store chains in the South. My family lived in such places as Live Oak and Orlando, Florida; and Valdosta, Tifton and Moultrie, Georgia. From that experience came a tale which he often related, about a boy and girl who were seated in the rumble seat of a parked car in the moonlight. When the boy asked if he might kiss the girl, she replied, "Piggly-Wiggly."

"What's this Piggly-Wiggly?" he asked.

"Hep yo-self!" was her reply.

My first memory of living in Thomasville centers around our residence at 318 Warren Avenue, to which we moved in 1934. The house had two bedrooms, a living and dining room, a kitchen, a center hall and a front and back porch. There was no bath within the house, so my father constructed a bath on the back porch. I shared the front bedroom with my sister, Nell, who was eleven years older than I, having been born on 22 October 1919 in Thomasville. There was a door that opened from our bedroom onto the front porch. When we wanted to use the bathroom and did not want to go through our parent's bedroom, we had to exit our bedroom onto the front porch, enter the house through the front door, exit the house through the back door and then enter the bathroom on the back porch. Having just moved into town from Aunt Annie's near Pavo, it was nice to have "indoor plumbing." My father also kept a cow tethered in the back yard, which furnished us milk as well as being our "lawn mower." How the cow was acquired is an interesting story. At that time, Georgia had no range laws so it was permissible to own livestock in town. My father learned that a milk cow was for sale in Pavo, so he and I went to see about purchasing her. When my father asked the owner if the cow was a good milk cow, he was told that she was a very good milk cow.

"How much milk will she give?", asked my father.

"She'll give all she can", replied the owner.

Now one cannot ask any more from a cow, can one?

Warren Avenue was not paved in 1934 and the dirt street served as a softball field. There were enough players, both boys and girls, in the neighborhood for several evening games each week during the summer months. My father usually did the pitching. My sister was an avid fan and a good player. At four and five years of age, I only watched. In 1936, I started to East Side Grammar School, the same year that my sister graduated from Thomasville High School, as the Class Valedictorian. Since our house was less than two blocks from the school, I usually walked to class each morning, stopping by the home of my maternal grandparents, Will and Hattie Shepherd, who lived around the corner from our home, at 120 Hansell Street. Incidentally, Joanne Woodward, the very talented and Academy Award winning actress, also was born in 1930, on Love Street around the corner from our Warren Avenue home. Joanne's father was the Principal at East Side Grammar School where we both began our education in 1936. In December of 1936, we moved from Warren Avenue to 407 North Crawford Street, only two houses from The Big Oak, one of Thomasville's main tourist attractions. We lived there until 1948 when I left home to attend West Point. My parents continued to live there until they divorced in 1950. Our house on Crawford Street is no longer standing. It was demolished by a next-door neighbor to make a parking lot which never materialized.

The Big Oak is a live oak (Quercus virginiana) and is truly a remarkable creation of God, while serving as a major tourist attraction within our City. The age of the tree is estimated to be in excess of three hundred, twenty-five years. Or to be more descriptive, when my emigrant ancestor arrived in Isle of Wight County, Virginia, in 1679, this oak was probably a seedling. The spread of the tree is 162 feet. Its height is 68 feet and its trunk circumference is 24 feet. Today, it is wired and braced to prevent the weight of its limbs from causing it to crash to the ground; but when we moved to our Crawford Street address in 1936, the City of Thomasville would decorate The Big Oak each Christmas Season with colored lights. As a child, I even climbed in the tree, which now, is strictly forbidden.

📖 📖 📖

Although I don't remember it, my maternal grandfather, William Walker Shepherd, had a summer cabin at Newport, Florida, a small fishing village on the Saint Marks River, a few miles from the Gulf of Mexico. The entire family began "going to Newport" in the late 1920s. The cabin was a four-room square building with a screened front porch, and was situated across the road from the sulphur springs at Newport. The cabin was visited each summer for many years, and I was told that I accompanied the family up until the time I was about three years old, in 1933, when vacations during the Depression were not feasible for our family. In later years, while visiting in Newport, Rhode Island, and seeing the "cottages" there, I jokingly told a group one evening that my family had had a cottage at Newport since the late 1920s!

📖 📖 📖

One of my most cherished memories of Crawford Street is how the City of Thomasville would occasionally block off traffic in the 400 block of Crawford in the evening during the summer months, so we neighborhood kids could roller skate. Our parents would bring their porch rocking chairs (not the folding kind) to the corners and sit under the street lights to chat and supervise the activity. I often wondered why our block was so honored. It did not occur to me until many years later that on our block lived the local Rabbi, and two members of the City hierarchy. We did have fun.

In the middle years of my Thomasville experiences, I had the "good fortune" to ride my bicycle each afternoon after school and all day on Saturday, delivering groceries to customers of our store, with their purchases loaded in an orange crate which was balanced on the handlebar of my bicycle. Occasionally, a one-, two-, or five-gallon can of kerosene for cook stoves was also slung over the handlebar. It was quite a balancing act. I only dumped my crate two times in all my years of apprenticeship. The positive aspect of those bicycle trips was an occasional, freshly-baked cookie. One of the negative aspects was getting wet while delivering in the rain. I also had to deliver to houses to which my colored co-deliverers would not go, "'cause that house is hainted." It did not matter that the house in question was currently lived in by live people. Once it got a reputation of being haunted, that was that. The fear of the dead, I have found, is not limited only to some colored folks; but my experiences with humorous events involving deaths or funerals are almost entirely derived from my early childhood in Thomas County, and many of the incidences revolved around my colored friends and their lives.

Each Saturday afternoon about six, my father would receive a written order from Mrs. Julia Haddock, who operated a restaurant down on West Jackson Street, "in the bottom", almost to the railroad tracks. The order was entirely for meat for her restaurant, to sustain her over the weekend. She never ordered by poundage, but always by dollar amounts: $1.00 worth of neck bones, $2.00 worth of spare ribs, 50 cents worth of beef scraps, $1.50 worth of round steak, etc. It was my privilege to deliver the order on my bicycle; because when I had deposited the items in her kitchen and had been paid in full in cash, I was seated at the "big table" in her kitchen where she prepared for me a hamburger patty between two slices of Flowers white bread, "slathered" with mayonnaise. What a treat it was to eat at that "special place" and have my meal personally prepared by Miss Julia. In later years, when I was invited to give a piano concert at the Cultural Center in Thomasville, I played an encore, a Scott Joplin "Rag", and dedicated it to Miss Julia, who was seated in the audience with her daughter. She had just celebrated her 100th birthday and was blind, but she appreciated the standing ovation she received that day.

In addition to the grocery and market my father operated in Thomasville, he owned and operated a farm south of Pavo. This was on land that had belonged to my father's mother, Alice; her sister, Aunt Annie; and their five brothers - Jim, Joe, John, Sam and William. As an aside, I found it interesting that three of the brothers had married ladies named Sallie. So the wives were differentiated by being called "Sallie Billy", "Sallie Jim" and "Sallie Sam." My father employed many colored workers, some of whom were share-croppers and some of whose families had been employed by my family for several generations. A few of the ancestors of the current workers had come to Georgia with my family from North Carolina in 1798. The relationship between employer and employees was quite good and many of my friends and playmates in my early years were colored. We would ride our bicycles together; we would shoot marbles together; and we would swim together down at "the swimming hole" or at Hart's pond near Aunt Annie's house, a short distance from Pavo. On one particular afternoon, several of us were at the pond. One of my colored playmates was not a very good swimmer and went out too far in the pond, panicked, and drowned before he could be rescued. His funeral was held a few days hence. Of course, my entire family was present and were seated on the second row of the church, just behind the "paid mourners." These were friends of the family who were paid a few dollars to sit on the front row of the church and "carry on" quite loudly in an attempt to "take some of the grief away from the family." During Johnny's funeral, one of the mourners cried out,

"Oh, Johnny, Johnny, jes speak to me one mo' time."

On the row behind my family, next to the window, sat a rotund colored lady with her young daughter, who responded to the mourner's lamentation:

"Effin he do, dis is mah winder."

Although I was born in Valdosta, I had traveled with my family to each of the Piggly-Wiggly sites noted previously (with the exception of Orlando, Florida); so, that by the time we moved to Thomasville, I possibly was the most well-traveled four-year-old in America! The last place we lived, and from where we moved to Thomasville, was Aunt Annie's house on Simmons Road, south of Pavo. This was a log house constructed about 1870, originally with two rooms on either side of a "dog trot" and a front and back porch. By 1930, the "dog trot" had been enclosed to make a hall in front and a dining room in the rear and the back porch had been screened. A well had been dug below the back porch, so that we had "indoor plumbing" even though the privy remained a considerable distance rearward of the house. A kitchen had been included on one end of the back porch and another bedroom had been added off the kitchen. A large fireplace warmed the parlor and another in the main bedroom which Aunt Annie occupied. This was a large room, approximately twenty feet square. Hanging in the ceiling was a quilting frame. On several occasions, I witnessed two or sometimes three ladies sitting around the lowered frame, quilting a newly-made bed covering. The ladies were guests in the house for several days until the quilt was finished. Then they would move on to another similar situation and perform their talents for another family. While I am sure they were fed and bedded down, I don't recall any money changing hands for their services. It's what families did for each other. It was a part of the bartering system prevalent in the South at that time. Also, on the wall of Aunt Annie's bedroom was a homemade telephone which her brothers had installed and connected to each of their homes. The telephone was attached to a large battery and, to make a call, a dial was set to the correct "number" and a crank was turned, ringing in the desired house.

In 1937, when the Rural Electrification Administration was created, my father wired Aunt Annie's home; and for Christmas that year, we all purchased light bulbs for her. She thanked us for the "new fangled contraptions" but continued to use mainly her Coleman lanterns and her Aladdin lamps.

Aunt Annie's place was a marvelous conglomeration of "goodies." In the immediate vicinity of the house, in what was designated "the yard", there were the following trees: pear, peach, orange, grapefruit, pomegranate, fig, tangerine, and kumquat and a grape arbor, all under towering pecan trees. There were also a smoke house and a corn crib. Immediately outward from the yard, was "the garden" which contained the usual vegetables grown in South Georgia: green peas, white peas, butter beans, pole beans, beets, tomatoes, butter squash, cantaloupes, watermelons, okra, corn and several kinds of herbs. Adjacent to the garden was the chicken yard where fowls of all kinds had free range: chickens, "biddies" and roosters, guineas, peafowl, ducks and geese. The requisite cats and dogs were also in attendance. Across Simmons Road, which ran in front of the house, were the barns which housed the cows, calves and bulls, the horses and mules, the pigs, and the farm equipment. Next to this collection of buildings was the sugar shelter under which the cane was put through the machine, as it was "turned" by a mule circling the site, and the juice was extracted and then funneled into the large heated iron boilers which cooked the liquid to make the cane syrup. Behind the sugar shelter was the mound of cane pumice, known as the "pummy" pile. It was a great treat to jump off the roof of the sugar shelter onto the pummy pile and roll down to the bottom. Of course, one had to be "nekkid" to enjoy this sticky treat, for clothes were too valuable to be soiled purposely.

When Aunt Annie died in 1945, only then did I realize just how much she had meant to my life. I spent many a wonderful time in her home. She could make the best ginger cookies I ever tasted; they were large, the size of a teacup (which she had used to cut them out), and sprinkled with flour after baking. The memory of Aunt Annie is kept alive in my current home on Warren Avenue, for on the mantle in my bedroom sits the same old oak kitchen clock which sat on the mantle in her bedroom. It had originally belonged to her parents, and had been ordered from the Sears & Roebuck catalog. I enjoy winding it every six days.

Over the years since I left Thomasville to attend West Point, I have often been asked about the "funny" Southern expression "y'all." This is really a simple and straight-forward colloquialism which causes many non-Southerners to appear perplexed when informed of its meaning. As a defining example, if one should meet another person on the street, engage that person in a brief or extended conversation, and then desire to invite that person to visit in one's home at a later date; one simply says,

"Y'all come see us."

If, however, one should meet two or more persons on the street, engage them in conversation, and then desire to invite all of them to visit one's home at a later date; one would say,

"All y'all come see us."

What's so funny about that?

Speaking of funerals, when I was about twelve years old, one of my mother's friends passed away. The deceased's funeral was held at the First Baptist Church in Thomasville with the Eastern Star grave-side service conducted at the Fredonia Baptist Church, a rural cemetery up-county. When the Church service was completed, my mother and several other Eastern Star members, assisted by several young helpers (guess who?), loaded the floral sprays in a station wagon and proceeded to the grave site ahead of the hearse and the family vehicles. When the "flower wagon" arrived at the grave site, all the helpers were unloading the flowers in a frenzy, attempting to complete the task before the family arrived. Just as the family limousine drew along side the grave site, one of the Eastern Star members, a petite lady wearing a hobble skirt, fell into the open grave. It was quite a sight to behold. I can only imagine what the family was witnessing, for I was dragged away in gales of laughter.

And speaking of laughter in Church situations, they were few in number but memorable in detail. At our First Baptist Church in Thomasville, when I was a youngster, the choir members did not wear robes. The ladies even wore their hats! My sister was often a soloist and, on one particular Sunday wore a new hat for the occasion. It was a brown felt, cone-shaped, Tyrolean creation with a small brush ornament on the band. True to the style of the times, my sister wore her hair in a "page boy", with a rubber band under her hair, to hold the hat on her head. She stood to present her solo; and as the organist, Mrs. Mabel Fleming, concluded the introduction, my sister opened her mouth to attack the first note. Simultaneously, the rubber band holding the hat on her head broke and the hat shot straight up in the air. Again, I can only imagine the full impact of this experience on the congregation for, once again, I was dragged from the sanctuary in convulsions of laughter.

Mrs. Fleming, the organist at our Church, was a talented musician and it was from her that I received my organ instructions. After taking lessons for about eighteen months, she allowed me to play, first for the Sunday evening services and then for the Sunday morning services. I shall later describe a wonderful opportunity she gave me just before my High School graduation.

On the 4th of July in 1942, my family drove down to Wakulla Springs, Florida, the source of the Wakulla River which flows southward into the Gulf of Mexico. At the Springs, there were glass-bottom boats which allowed the viewers to see the "trained" fish, Henry, jump over a sunken pole; and to watch a coin descend to the bottom, some 160 feet down. I do believe the water is the coldest I have ever experienced. A tower had been recently erected so that either divers or jumpers could enter the water from both the thirty- and the forty-foot levels. On this particular day, a "Tarzan" movie was being filmed. My sister asked the star, Johnny Weissmuller, if she could take his picture. I have a copy of that snapshot, taken at the bottom of the tower, of that great Olympic swimmer in his black "Speedo." He had won Olympic Gold Medals in both 1924 and 1928 in the 100-Meter Freestyle Event, as well as the 1924 Gold Medal in the 400-Meter Freestyle Event. I remember him to have been a most friendly and cooperative celebrity. It was also a treat to have witnessed the filming of a movie, even though I do not remember the name of the film.

Some Southern expressions appear to be polite substitutions, or just words that sound like other words. For example, instead of saying "I'll swear", a Southerner might say "I'll swanee", possibly influenced by the nearness of the Suwanee River which originates in the Okefenokee Swamp in southeastern Georgia and flows through Florida to the Gulf of Mexico. To expand that expression, instead of saying "I'll swear to God", it comes out as "I'll swan to goodness." I have heard this latter expression since my earliest childhood days, for having been raised rather strictly in the Baptist heritage, I was instructed early on that one does not use the name of the Lord in any fashion which might possibly be construed to be disrespectful.

My paternal great-grandmother, Martha Hancock Sherrod, originated the idea for the founding of the Salem Baptist Church south of Pavo. It was her husband's father, William Sherrod, who gave the land to the Church. In that Church, in the earliest days, and continuing into my childhood, the men sat on one side of the Church and the women and children sat on the other. In later years of study, I realized how similar the Southern Baptist religion and customs paralleled those of the Jewish religion. In fact, while living in the Maryland suburbs of Washington, DC, during the 1980s, I would occasionally visit the Jewish Community Center near our home and play recreational piano music for the elderly residents. On one particular occasion, as I was playing some Broadway show tunes, an elderly lady approached me with her walker. As she forcibly removed my hands from the keyboard, she said,

"You don't look Jewish."

I replied, "I'm not; I'm a South Georgia Baptist."

"Vell", she said, "That's almost as good."

On several occasions, my family attended Temple B'nai Israel in Thomasville. We were truly ecumenical, or more accurately, curious, if the truth be told. I was always interested in the varied religious services about which I had read, and I have attended as many different ones as possible throughout my life and travels. In fact, after we were married, my wife and I attended services at The New York Avenue Presbyterian

Church in Washington, DC; Faith Methodist, Seven Locks Road Baptist and Saint Elizabeth's Catholic Churches in Rockville and Bethesda, Maryland; The Old Dutch Reformed Church in Kingston, New York; the Church of Saint John the Divine in New York City; The National Cathedral of Saints Peter and Paul in Washington, DC; and both the First Baptist and Saint Thomas Episcopal Churches in Thomasville. In my travels, I have attended services at the American Church in Paris, France, and several places of worship in the Arab world. As a teenager, I was often a guest organist at the St. Augustine Catholic Church in Thomasville, and possibly I am the only South Georgia Baptist who can sing all of "Tantum Ergo, Sacramentum" in Latin!

As I have previously stated, my father had sixty first cousins. One of them, Annabel Horn, was Dean of Students at Wesleyan Conservatory of Music in Macon, Georgia. In 1935, my family drove from Thomasville to Macon to visit with Cousin Annabel during Commencement Week at the Conservatory. On the afternoon of our visit to her office, two former students at the Conservatory dropped by to say hello to their former Dean. We were all introduced to two young Chinese ladies, Ching-ling and Mei-ling Soong, who in later years married, respectively, the two great Chinese leaders, Sun Yat-sen and Chiang Kai-shek. Madame Chiang was born in 1898 and was a staunch ally of the United States during the Second World War. She died in New York City in 2003, at the age of 105 years.

My wife, Chase, and I were married in St. Thomas Episcopal Church in Thomasville; and on each visit to that church, both before and after our marriage, I was always encouraged to kneel. My excuses were, first, that we Baptists did not kneel in our Church. Then I protested that my Army uniform trousers were creased and could not be blemished. When Chase attended the Baptist services with me, I always encouraged her to stand and be recognized as a visitor. Neither of us was ever successful in our attempts, but we always tried.

My First Baptist pastor, Reverend Timothy Furlough Callaway, was a great influence in my life. He was instrumental in gathering together, in late 1947, at the Plaza café in Thomasville, my father and my Congressman, Judge Eugene E. Cox, who represented the Second District of Georgia in the United States House of Representatives. As I joined that threesome by invitation, on a weekday afternoon in my Senior Year in high school, the result was an appointment to the United States Military Academy, the critical juncture in my career path. I admired Preacher Callaway very much for his knowledge of the Bible. However, his delivery was somewhat difficult - he "snapped" his words crisply. His nickname, even to his face by some, was "Brother Snap."

Reverend Callaway had a running dialogue of good humor with the Methodist Minister in Thomasville, Reverend Mack Anthony. On many occasions from the pulpit, he would regale the congregation with a recent event in their association. One Sunday, he reported that Brother Anthony had told him that, on the previous Sunday, a lady had joined the Methodist Church but had requested that she be baptized like a Baptist

-- immersion versus sprinkling -- and that Brother Anthony had asked him if he would do the honors.

"I told Brother Anthony," said Brother Snap,
"that I don't take in washin', but that I'd
loan him my tub."

My teenage years in Thomasville were highlighted by many memorable events and experiences. I particularly remember my association with Miss Marie Wertz - a teacher of extraordinary talent, but one with a definite Germanic mien, who considered and vocally labeled each of her students who made an error in class as "a silly goose." Miss Wertz taught classes in mathematics -- algebra, plane and solid geometry, and trigonometry –- and Latin. She always encouraged her students to strive for perfection in all things; and for a few of us who were particularly interested in exploring the mathematical unknown, she not only encouraged us but took time after the school hours to assist us in our pursuits. My interest was in plane geometry. She pointed out that there were three problems that were insolvable: the quadrature of the circle, the duplication of the cube, and the trisection of an angle. The latter intrigued me even though I knew it was impossible. I asked Miss Wertz if there existed any close approximations. She replied that there were none but if I was interested, I should try my hand at an attempt. This project lasted most of my Junior Year, with many visits to the home of Miss Wertz in the late afternoon or early evening, to show her my progress. She seemed delighted in my pursuit and encouraged me with helpful suggestions along the way. The result was a geometric construction with an algebraic "proof" which pointed out the impossibility of the task but also my close approximation to the solution, which made my efforts usable for practical purposes. I was pleased to receive for my efforts, on 1 June 1947, a Copyright, Class 1, UNP. No. 2948, issued by The Copyright Office of the United States Library of Congress. Miss Wertz seemed genuinely pleased that the efforts of one of her students had been so acknowledged. In later years, I was able to program my efforts on an IBM 709 computer, and demonstrated that the error was only 0 degrees, 21 minutes, and 40 seconds at an angle of 90 degrees. For acute angles (less than 90 degrees), the error was proportionately smaller. This result was published in the <u>American Mathematical Journal</u>, Volume 68, No. 9, in November, 1961.

In my Junior Year in High School, I was a member of the Kiwanis- sponsored Key Club. At the State of Georgia Key Club convention, held in Macon in 1947, I was elected to the Post of State Secretary. The next year, as a Delegate to Boys' State, I was elected to the post of Georgia State Attorney General.

📖 📖 📖

In the summer of 1947, between my Junior and Senior Years, I accompanied my maternal grandparents, Will and Hattie Shepherd, on a train trip from Thomasville to New York City, to visit their youngest son and his family, who were then living in Bergenfield, New Jersey. Uncle Joe was a Chief Petty Officer stationed at the Brooklyn Navy Yard. It was the first time that either Papa, Big Mama or I had ever been that far North. We boarded a train in Thomasville and traveled eastward to Nahunta, Georgia, where we changed trains. We boarded "The Champion", the Atlantic Coast Line's "Superliner" which made daily runs from Miami, Florida, to New York City, and return. We had only purchased Coach Seats, so we "sat up" all night. Even if we had purchased "sleeper" accommodations, it would have been a waste of money, for I looked out the window almost the entire trip. When we arrived at Pennsylvania Station in New York City, Uncle Joe met us and drove us to his home in New Jersey. It was a fantastic drive across the George Washington Bridge. I was in total amazement! While my grandparents were content to stay at Uncle Joe's every day, I wanted to venture out and do some sight-seeing on my own. One morning, Uncle Joe accompanied me as we took the bus from Bergenfield to Manhattan, getting off at 180th Street. We then took a subway train downtown to Times Square. After a brief walk around the area, we took another subway train down to The Battery, where we then took a ferry boat out to The Statue of Liberty. We ascended the Statue in the elevator all the way to the crown. The 360-degree view of the area was almost breathtaking. After we had returned to Manhattan and boarded an "uptown train", we exited the subway at 34th Street and bought sight-seeing tickets to the top of The Empire State Building. When our tour was completed, and we were standing on the 86th Floor awaiting the "down" elevator; as the doors opened, the first person out of the car was Dr. Herbert F. Readling, our family physician in Thomasville. He was in New York for a Medical Convention. Small world, indeed. On successive days, I was allowed to make that same trip from Bergenfield to New York City by myself, and did so three or four times. I really felt mature. How or why my parents allowed a seventeen-year old, who had never been that far "away from home" before, to venture on his own, I could never understand. But it was a wonderful experience, one that I have always remembered fondly.

There is one event in my high school career that stands out in my memory as an example of the question, "Could this really have happened to me?" During my Junior Year, I tried out for the track team, and ran the hurdles. On this particular day, I traveled by car (someone else's) with three other guys to Camilla, a town some forty miles north of Thomasville, for a track meet. The event's outcome is not important, and I have forgotten the details. However, after the meet, a dance was held in the Camilla High School gymnasium. This lasted for several hours, so by the time it was over, the time was near midnight. The four of us started home, and, on the outskirts of Camilla, our vehicle had a blowout -- not just a flat tire, but a blowout! And wouldn't you know it! We did not have a spare. So we sat on the Camilla-Thomasville highway, at about one in the morning, waiting for another driver to come by, to offer assistance. Remember, this is 1947. Traffic was not heavy on that highway at that time of the early morning. Finally, a pick-up truck came by. The driver had a spare which he lent us, but followed us to Thomasville to insure that he got back his spare. When I finally arrived at my home, my mother was sitting in the living room, reading, with all the lights on. As I walked in, she inquired if I had had a good time. I then proceeded to tell her the entire episode, to which she responded, "Why didn't you call?" My response was, "Mother, we don't have a telephone." (We didn't get a telephone in our home until the Spring of my Senior Year, and it was a four-party line!) Not to be outdone, mother then said, "Well, you could have called "No-eh" (Noah Stegall was Thomasville's Chief of Police and a good friend of the family) and he would have come and told me where you were." It was of no consequence to tell her that there were no phones on that road at that hour. Her final remark was, "Don't ever do that again."

After graduating from High School, I had planned to attend Columbia University in New York City to study mathematics, particularly since I had heard nothing from West Point since taking my physical and mental examinations in February, 1948. While getting dressed on Sunday, the 30th of May, for the Baccalaureate Service at the First Baptist Church, a Western Union man on a bicycle brought me a telegram which said, "Report to West Point on 1 July for entry into The United States Military Academy." That was that.

After I got to West Point, I read in detail about the first black graduate of the Military Academy, Henry Ossian Flipper, who had graduated in 1877. He was born a slave in Thomasville. I already knew about Henry Flipper, for, as a youngster of about nine or ten, I had been introduced by my father to Henry's youngest brother, Festus, a blind cobbler who operated a shoe repair shop on South Broad Street. Festus told me quite a bit about his brother, Henry, and how he had been "cashiered" out of the Army on trumped up charges. After graduating from West Point in 1952, I became aware of the efforts of a South Georgia school teacher, Ray McColl, who had undertaken a seemingly impossible task to have the records reviewed, expunged, and corrected to reflect the rightful place in the annals of the United States Army to which Henry Flipper deserved to be remembered. After many years of untiring effort, Ray McColl was successful in doing what he had set out to do. The Army corrected all the records, absolved Henry Flipper of all the charges made against him, and returned his name to the place of honor to which the First Black Graduate of West Point deserved. As a final gesture of respect, Henry Flipper's remains were disinterred from the Atlanta, Georgia, cemetery where they had resided for many years, and were re-interred in Thomasville in a ceremony with honor and distinction. It will always give me great pleasure to remember that I was honored to speak as the representative of the United States Military Academy and of the Association of Graduates of West Point at those church and re-interment services. A Federal marker now stands on Madison Street near the grave sites of Henry and his parents.

📖 📖 📖

Thomasville has always held fond memories for me, memories from my earliest days in 1934, when we moved "in town" from Pavo, until I left to attend West Point in 1948. From the time I could ride a bicycle, I was "invited" to help out at my father's store. There are many stories associated with the store, but one of the funniest involved the rationing of food during World War II. There were many items which were scarce during that period of history -- soap and soap powders, cooking oil, catsup, coffee, sugar, coconut, canned pineapple, and many others. My father devised a "code system" for his "special" customers, so that during periods of much store activity, a special customer could inquire about the existence of a scarce item without the entire customer population being informed. The code name for coffee was "dog food." On one particular Saturday afternoon, the store was full of customers. One special customer, Mrs. Della Golden, walked in and asked if we had gotten in any "dog food." My father turned to Henry, one of the young colored boys who worked just on Saturdays, and instructed him to get Mrs. Golden "a pound of dog food." Henry went behind one of the counters, rumbled around nosily, stuck his head up over the edge of the counter, and inquired,

"Is yo' dog regular or does he drip?"

The store exploded in laughter.

Another incident involving shortages occurred when a lady came in the store and asked if we had any breakfast bacon. When my father replied that we did, she asked the price.

"Thirty-five cents a pound", was the reply.

She responded, "I've just come from Mr. Dixon's across the street, and he sells his for thirty cents a pound, but he's out."

My father replied, "Well, if I didn't have any, mine would be twenty-five cents."

Some of the fondest memories of my childhood are the relationships that existed among the people of Thomasville, relationships of service to each other, always helping out and doing for others. As one example, when the Southern Bell Telephone office was upstairs over McClelland's Ten Cent (Variety) Store on Broad Street, one morning my mother picked up the phone at our store and asked the operator if she had seen her "mama", Mrs. Shepherd. I can just visualize the sequence of events: the operator, Mrs. Hattie Johnson, removed her headset, walked to the window, looked up the street, came back to the switchboard, readjusted her headset, and reported,

"She's jes' goin' in Neel's. I'll ring."

On several occasions, customers of our store would ask if we could go over to Neel's Department Store, purchase a specific spool of thread or a skein of wool, or some other notion, deliver it with the groceries, and charge the entire lot for thirty days. Of course we did. Wouldn't everyone?

My father kept our store open, when it was first located at 209 West Jackson Street, from six in the morning until seven at night during the week and until midnight on Saturdays. After we had finished cleaning up the store each Saturday, we would then go across the street to the Greek-American Restaurant to have a bite to eat, even though it probably was then close to one o'clock on Sunday morning. On one particular visit to the restaurant, I overheard a conversation at the counter, when a farmer in overalls asked the waitress for "a cup o' coffee an' a piece o' pie."

"What kinda pie you want?", asked the waitress.

"'Tater pie, woman. Doncha know what pies are made out of?"

Remember, this was the late 1930s and sweet potato pie was then quite common in the South.

"Fixin' to go," "aimin' to do that," "rarin' to beat the band," and similar expressions are quite common in the South. When challenged by my Northern friends on such terminologies, I usually counter with the query "How can one bring you to the Church on Sunday? Why not 'carry'?" But then I am confronted with "I'm jes' plum tuckered" (tired), and have no response. Another combination of words, "I got to have..." for "I need to have..." is also quite common. And when someone acts peculiar or not quite normal, one might say that he or she is "not insane, just turned funny." Then it falls to the speaker to identify "funny" as in "funny ha ha" or "funny peculiar."

My grandmother Shepherd had a visitor one day who was passing through Thomasville on her way to Florida. The visitor and my grandmother had not seen each other for quite some time. They visited in "the parlor" past sunset. Emma, the major-domo of my grandmother's household, appeared in the doorway.

"Emma, of course Mrs. Martin will be staying for supper and overnight. We have plenty of food and lots of room, don't we?", inquired my grandmother.

"Yassum," replied Emma. "We can sleep twelve and eat any number."

Every town has its modern Mrs. Malaprop, and Thomasville was no exception. However, there were several individuals who could arguably vie for that honor. On one particular occasion, Katie CoCroft, whose husband, Chris, had just been hospitalized for eye surgery, came into Neel's and was confronted by one such individual, Mrs. Essie Baker, the local milliner.

"I hear that Chris has had surgery," said Miss Essie.

"Yes he has," was the reply. "He had a detached retina, but we don't believe his eyesight will be adversely affected."

"Something wrong with his eyes too?", asked Miss Essie.

On another occasion, this same Mrs. Baker arrived for work on the Monday following Easter. Beautifully arranged on the top of the front counter in the store was a large vase of Easter lilies.

"Oh, what a beautiful vase of lilies, so pure and white. They remind me of Jesus, Moses, and Elias on the Cross."

Mrs. Baker was quite the millinery connoisseuse and prided herself on being "up-to-date" on the latest Paris fashions. On one occasion, after showing several of her "creations" to a customer, she said,

"This is the latest hat from Paris."

Looking at the label inside, the customer responded,

"This says 'Made in Czechoslovakia'."

"Yes," replied Mrs. Baker, "That's the finest hat shop in Paris."

📖 📖 📖

Over the years, I have marveled at the relative costs of items in the mid-thirties versus the current era. I realize that it isn't a fair comparison and that much has changed since I was a child; but I can't help being fascinated by reminiscing, especially when I attend a movie in New York City and must pay as much as ten dollars, or sometimes more. As late as 1940, a child under twelve could attend the Rose Theater in Thomasville for nine cents. Adult tickets were only thirty-five cents. I recall that on Saturday, after raking the yard around our home on Crawford Street and being paid thirty-five cents for my labor, I would go to the afternoon show at the Rose to see an "oater", a Flash Gordon serial (sometimes on green film), a Pete Smith specialty, two or three cartoons, and perhaps "The Sons of the Pioneers" to boot, all for nine cents. Popcorn was a nickel, as was a candy bar. I never bought a candy bar for the afternoon performance since I usually took one with me from my father's store for the evening performance at the Mode Theater on Broad Street, where the program was similar. The colored folks had their own theater, the Ritz, located down in "the Bottom." There was a fourth theater in town: the Hiwa, a drive-in, farther out on Jackson Street. Just imagine: four theaters in a town of eighteen thousand! Wow! When I would get out of the evening movie, I would stop by the barber shop, across from our store on West Jackson Street, for a five cent shoe shine, so that I would be presentable at Sunday School and Church the next morning. After putting five cents in the collection plate at Church (my tithe), I had two cents left for my savings bank which sat on my bedroom dresser. As I got older and was afforded the "privilege" of delivering groceries on my bicycle, my weekly allowance climbed to one dollar for a weekday afternoon's work and two dollars for working all day Saturday. For a teenager in Thomasville in the 40s, those were "big bucks."

One of my favorite relatives was my great-uncle Joe Sherrod, another of Aunt Annie's brothers. Similar to the actions of his mother, Martha, regarding Salem Church, Uncle Joe founded Antioch Church south of Pavo. He was a man of immense physical proportions with "a heart of gold" but lacking in any formal education. His land holdings in Thomas County were extensive; he was considered by one and all as a most successful business man. I always enjoyed visiting Uncle Joe at his "place" with my father each time we went out to Aunt Annie's, but I enjoyed more Uncle Joe visiting us, for he always gave me a dollar bill on each visit. Uncle Joe always managed to arrive at our home in time for dinner. On one particular occasion, as he served himself from the platter before him, he inquired as to the nature of his meal.

"They're cod fish balls," said my mother.

"Well, they're mighty good. I'll have another pair," replied my favorite uncle.

In the Baptist community near Pavo where my father was raised, dancing was strictly prohibited. However, when folks gathered for a large party or a Church social, the "orchestra" consisted of several "fiddles" (violins played at a lower angle); a string tub (a galvanized wash tub inverted, with a wire attached to a pole placed thereon); and perhaps a jug or two (considered wind instruments because the player blew across the top of the jug). Since music was provided and music sometimes makes people move in rhythm, the young folks would form a circle, with each couple therein holding hands at arm's length. This was not dancing; it was called "twisterfication." A rose by any name...

Several "nonsense" songs have remained in my memory, songs which were taught to me by my parents and grandparents. The words had little or no meaning, as long as the lines rhymed. After all, they were "nonsense" songs. One in particular stands out. It was called "Lady Bonner-rink-tum." It goes like this:

> "What we gonna have for the wed-ding sup-per?
> Lady Bonner-rink-tum kind-beau.
> Three green peas all stewed in but-ter.
> Lady Bonner-rink-tum kind-beau.
> Kigh-muh-nay-ro, Cap-ten Kay-ro,
> Kigh-muh-nay-ro, kind-beau,

Lady Bonner-rink-tum, som-a-nick-er, dom-a-nick-er,
Lady Bonner-rink-tum kind-beau."

This style of poetry will probably never qualify as "noteworthy", but it has remained in my memory for decades, and represents the "times during The Depression" when people created their own entertainment, at little or no cost.

Everything is relative. My maternal grandfather Shepherd used to say that

"All money is relative. The more money you have, the more relatives."

By no stretch of the imagination could my family have been considered "well off." However, we did own land in rural Thomas County, on which quite a bit of produce was grown to supply my father's grocery store. During the 1930s, and even into the early 40s, bartering was the norm among many families in Thomas County and throughout the South. My father ran "annual accounts" for many farmers and their families, providing them with staples, some meat, and other necessities during the year, until the first Saturday after the first frost in November. That was the agreed-upon date for "hog-killin'." During the butchering of hogs, the saying was that everything was saved except the squeal! The blood was used to make blood pudding. The heads were used in hog head cheese. The feet were pickled. The ears were boiled, and the intestines became chitterlings, or to be more precisely Southern, "chitlins."

All during the year, the farmers would bring my father eggs, smoked hams, jars of pickled or preserved fruits and vegetables, home-made brooms, scuppernong grape wine (for medicinal purposes, only!) and anything else that might reduce their indebtedness. Then, on a Saturday in late November, "the day of reckoning" would arrive and the annual conversation would sound something like this:

"Well, Mr. R., what do I owe you this year?"

"Looks like about five dollars this time."

"Well, jes' put that on next year's tab."

Money seldom changed hands in these transactions, or for that matter, in allied transactions, as well. Sometimes my mother would take one of the smoked hams, which had arrived during the year as a partial debt payment, across the street to a dry-goods store, to exchange for a bolt of cloth, which she then took to a seamstress, usually my maternal grandmother, to have a new dress made for herself and/or my sister. Upon the completion of the new dress(es), the seamstress might get some groceries from our store or perhaps a little money or a combination of the two.

Bartering was a way of life in the South in which both sides knew, or agreed upon readily, the cost of the items being swapped. When my father decided to add another bedroom to our home on Crawford Street and to redo the kitchen, he negotiated with a well-known and beloved colored man, Alec Hayes, quite advanced in years, but still in his prime for carpentry. The agreed-upon price for the entire job, at a pace to be set by the carpenter, was groceries and meat for one entire year, for the carpenter and his wife, my father supplying all the building materials which he had bartered with a local lumber company to prepare, the pine trees having been cut from our place near Pavo.

Friends have always been important in my life. I suppose I had the best training in this department from my parents. My father befriended literally everyone with whom he came in contact. In 1944, my father was hospitalized in Archbold Memorial Hospital in Thomasville with double pneumonia. During the three weeks he was absent from our store, now located at 110 East Jackson Street, five local butchers, all in competition with our store, took turns cutting meat at our store so that our regular customers would not suffer in my father's absence.

My father also seemed to be attracted to the "down-trodden." There was one such person in Thomasville who never seemed to have anything nice. His clothes were shoddy. He was never clean-shaven. He spent most of his waking hours just walking the streets and visiting with what few friends he had. After many years of such predictable activity, the man died. He had instructed a lawyer friend to have his funeral service at the grave site in Laurel Hill Cemetery at two o'clock in the morning! My father opined that there would probably not be very many at his funeral, so he, my father, ought to attend. This he did, together with one other man. The two of them comprised the entire group of "mourners." The lawyer was also in attendance and, after the brief interment ceremony, he informed my father and the other man that the deceased had left a modest estate to be divided equally among those persons attending his grave-side ceremony. I never learned how much money was involved, for my father gave his share to Preacher Callaway at the First Baptist Church.

Thomasville has been known as a winter retreat for many decades. The settling of the community did not begin with the late Nineteenth century, however. When I first became interested in the history of the area, I learned from one of Thomasville's earliest and finest historians, Miss Bessie Hopkins, that Hernando De Soto had spent the winter of 1539-1540 at Anhayca, between Tallahassee, Florida, and Thomasville, Georgia. While this may be a stretch to be called "the beginning of the tourist trade", it has always fascinated me to know of this early history. It is not a stretch to say that the area around Thomasville has been visited by foreigners since the 16th Century! However, the real influx of Northerners began in the late Nineteenth Century. I use the term "Northerners" meaning anyone from outside the limits of Thomas County on the Moultrie Road! My grandmother Shepherd used to say that anyone north of Atlanta needed a Visa. (She was born in 1874!) Thomasville has always accepted newcomers to the community, both readily and graciously, with some rare, unintentional slights. I recall visiting my mother in her ninetieth year and having her refer to a family "over on Park front", meaning, of course, that area of Hansell Street facing Paradise Park. When I was unable to remember the family in question due to the fact that I had been away from Thomasville for more than forty years, my mother said:

"Of course you remember them. They're that new family that came here in '22."

Oh, well. So much for local residency requirements.

Schooling for me has always been of great interest. I still am fascinated by the acquisition of knowledge. Growing up in Thomasville's school system was the beginning of a lifetime of learning, and I have often marveled at the depth and quality of the education I received. Starting at East Side Grammar School, now the Thomasville Cultural Center, in 1936, in the first grade, taught by Miss Daisy Neel, I learned to work with others in the construction of a "playhouse" that had real wall paper and "hinged" cardboard doors. We also got to feed Henry, the goldfish, and to use our crayon boxes for whatever purposes seemed expedient. Miss Edna Fort taught the second grade and Miss Ruth Burch, the third. Miss Evelyn Smith was our fourth grade teacher and Miss Beth Terry, a niece of Dr. Terry at the Drug Store of the same name, taught the fifth. In the sixth grade, taught by Miss Mamie Milner, we put on an Easter Pageant in the school auditorium. It was so well received that we were invited to re-present it at The First Baptist Church. This was my first association with "the stage" and its theatrical aspects which would later bring me in contact with some of the great performers in the world.

On Friday, in the evening of the 5th day of April in the year 1940, I accepted Jesus Christ as my Lord and Savior in a Revival Service at The First Baptist Church in Thomasville. The Minister conducting the Service was The Reverend Luther Holcomb. As the congregation sang the Hymn of Invitation, "Pass Me Not, Oh Gentle Savior", I walked down the aisle and asked Him to come into my life. I was baptized in the Pool of the Church on Sunday Night, 21 April 1940, by Reverend

Luther J. Holcomb, the father of the guest Minister. On Friday, 26 April 1940, I received a copy of The Scofield Reference Bible, with a "penny post card" which said in part: "I am glad that you came into the church during the recent revival, and I want you to know that a friend of mine, Mr. Maxey Jarman, is sending you a Bible. Mr. Jarman and I read through the Bible each year, reading four chapters each day. Luther J. Holcomb Nashville, Tennessee". Enclosed with the Bible was a printed card from "The Jarman Foundation, J.F. Jarman, Founder, Maxey Jarman, Trustee." (In later years, when I had returned from the Korean War and was stationed in Nashville, I called on the Jarman Family and was introduced to their son, Claude, who had played the major role in the movie, "The Yearling.")

Inscribed on the opening page of this Bible are several verses written by my mother:

"In all thy ways acknowledge Him and He will direct thy paths." Proverbs 3:6.

"Create in me a clean heart, O God; and renew a right spirit within me." Psalm 51:10.

"Greater is He who is in you, than he who is in the world." I John 4:4.

"Therefore all things whatsoever ye would that men should do to you, do ye even so to them..." Matthew 7:14.

This Bible has been used over the years so that it now is frayed around its edges; but all of its pages, although many are loose, are still in place.

I finally "retired" it from daily use in 1999 when I received from a friend in California a copy of The MacArthur Study Bible of the New King James Version.

Speaking of the King James Version of the Bible, I have contended, since 1951, that the King James Version of the Bible was "written", or the writing was coordinated, by William Shakespear. I came to this conclusion while I was lying in a hospital bed in the West Point Infirmary, recuperating from the mumps. I discovered, being the sleuth in mathematics that I am, that, since Shakespear was born in 1564; in the year 1610, he was forty-six years of age. The King James Version of the Bible was completed in 1610, although it was not published until 1611. If one looks at Psalm 46 and begins to count the words from the beginning, the 46th word is "shake." If one counts from the end of the Psalm, the 46th word is "spear." (The word "SELAH" is probably a notational musical instruction which appears often throughout The Psalms. It is not a part of the text.) How's that for sleuthing?

In 1942, when I graduated to the seventh grade and walked with my class from East Side Grammar School down the hill to MacIntyre Park Junior High, I remember feeling a sense of "growing up." This is when we had a home room teacher and then traveled to a different room for each subject. What a novelty! "Miss Mashburn from Ashburn" was our seventh grade home room teacher. Then came the eighth. Mrs. Evie Milton decided that, after having us for one year, she would like to do it again. So she was our ninth grade home room teacher. She then said that she enjoyed us so much, she would like to follow us through the rest of our High School days. And she did, being our home room teacher in the tenth, eleventh, and twelfth years. Along the way, we received wonderful instruction from Miss Marjorie Love in French and Latin; Mr. Ben Nunn taught us Chemistry; Mr. Thomas McComb, the High School Principal, whose favorite expression was "horribile dictu", taught us Physics; Miss Marjorie Stith taught us Bible (then a part of the school curriculum); Miss Elise Gannon was our instructress in Literature and Shakespear; and Miss Patty Ruth Britt taught us Civics and American Government. However, the one teacher who stands out as the highlight of my High School education was Miss Marie Wertz who taught me Algebra, Plane and Solid Geometry, and Trigonometry. Miss Wertz had received her Masters Degree in Mathematics from Columbia University. Her thesis was proving the Pythagorean Theorem a new way. She held the distinction of being only the second person in the world to have accomplished this task, the first being United States President James Abram Garfield.

I was not a discipline problem to my parents while I was in school but I did have a few escapades which required the suspension of some privileges, confinement to my room, or on rare occasions, I was directed by my mother to retrieve from a bush in the yard a "switch" which was promptly applied to my derrière. However, there is one episode that needs to be mentioned, for it was the only time in my entire life that my father used his belt on me. What occasioned this incident was a comment that I made to a teacher when I was in the eighth grade. She had quite properly disciplined me for something that I had or had not done, I don't remember which. But it was the "or else" comment that she made that really got to me, and I replied, "oh, yeah." I thought no more about it until I got home that afternoon after track practice. My father was sitting on the front steps. As I approached him, he quite calmly inquired if I had "sassed" a teacher in school that day. I thought about my answer long and hard, only because quite frankly I had forgotten the incident until he reminded me. "Did you say to your teacher 'oh yeah'?", he inquired. When I admitted that I had, he reminded me quite sternly that when I was in school, the teachers spoke for him and my mother; and that whatever they instructed me to do, I should accept it as though the command had come from one of them. He then invited me to accompany him into the bathroom where I was instructed to lower my trousers and my underwear and bend over the tub. I then was invited to remove his belt from his trousers so that he could apply it appropriately. The belt made quite an impression on me, literally as well as figuratively. After several applications to my derrière, the belt was handed to me and I was told to put it back around my father's waist. He further stated that he did not ever expect to have to use it again in a similar manner. I assured him that he never would. And he never did.

In 1942, as America was getting into mobilization for the Second World War, the Department of Civil Defense was establishing all over America what came to be known as "Filter Centers." These were operations set up to locate and track all aircraft flying over the coastal areas of the United States. Spotting towers were manned during daylight hours by personnel with telephones, who, when a plane was sighted, called into the switchboard with a "report of sighting." Depending on the location of the tower, the call was routed to one of several persons around a large map of the area, each having a long-handled "rake" used for the placing, movement or retrieval of the small plane models. The person in the tower would indicate the type of plane, its direction, estimated speed and any other data deemed to be important. The map board was about three feet off the floor and covered almost the entire main room of the fifth floor of the Upchurch Building, the only five-story building in Thomasville. The area covered by the Thomasville sector was a major portion of south Georgia and the upper third of Florida. In early 1943, I applied for work as a volunteer. Even though I was only "about to be thirteen", I was big for my age and had a recommendation from the principal at the High School, saying that he thought I could handle almost any assignment given me. My first and only job was as a telephone operator. I went to the Filter Center three times each week after school for three hours, for almost two years. I really felt that I was doing something patriotic on the home front and serving my country well.

During my High School years, it seemed to me that I spent an inordinate amount of time in the dentist's chair. (At that time, City water did not contain any fluoride.) Our family dentist was Dr. William M. Searcy, Jr. "Dr. Bill" was an excellent practitioner but my threshold of pain was severely challenged on many occasions. It was for that reason, I believe, that I was assigned to Dr. Bill's new Assistant, Dr. Ben Grace, when he arrived on the scene. By the time I graduated from High School, Dr. Ben had filled just about every tooth in my head. In later years, while living in Chevy Chase, Maryland, in the rented house of a Russian widow, I began using the services of her son and his assistant, who, over about ten years, replaced with gold all the amalgam fillings put in by Ben Grace except one, which I kept for "sentimental" reasons. I am proud to report that the one amalgam I saved is still in tact, margins and all. Incidentally, Ben Grace later served as the chief usher in my wedding.

In 1911, my maternal grandfather, William Walker Shepherd, bought one of the first two Ford automobiles which arrived in Thomasville. A Mr. Stanaland purchased the other one. Papa, as he was known by his grandchildren, drove this seven-passenger touring car, with its isinglass (mica) curtains and its horse-hair-stuffed leather cushions, for several years. The car was a participant in several parades in both Thomasville and Valdosta but sometime after 1925, Papa, then living in Valdosta, built a brick garage and "sealed" the car in mausoleum fashion because he had purchased a newer Model A. When I was a Junior in High School, in mid-1947, some other members of the family persuaded Papa to "sell" me the car for one dollar. The garage was opened and the car was "exhumed." Of course, the tires had long ago rotted, so I wrote to the Ford Motor Company and got a new set of tires. Alec Hayes, the colored carpenter who had worked on our kitchen renovation, was also a very good automobile mechanic. The Ford was taken to his shop on Madison Street, across from the American Legion Post 31 building, and he proceeded to "bring it up to snuff." The klaxon horn, which had not been electrified in 1911, received a new rubber bulb. The brass lanterns and the connecting rods from the middle of the windshield to the front bumpers, were shined; and the headlights, which shone brighter the faster one drove, were also polished. The windshield was made in two sections and folded down. The crank under the radiator had a mind of its own. Whenever one tried to "start" the car, one had to be certain to let go of the crank after a few revolutions, or receive a severe, possibly arm-breaking backlash. The car was ready for use in the Fall of 1947 and became quite a "hit" at school. Another student had an old "station wagon", and our two vehicles were usually the modes of transportation for lunch-break excursions or after-school visits to Terry's Drug Store on Broad Street. After I left for West Point, my father sold the car. Although I have not seen it, I am told that it is now on display at the Antique Auto Museum near Stone Mountain, Georgia.

In 1947, The Junior Service League put on what has become a tradition in Thomasville: the first "Follies." Although I was only seventeen, I was a big seventeen who loved to dance. The show was staged in the Municipal Auditorium under the guidance of a New York choreographer. The Chorus, or "Hoofers", were composed of eight men and eight women, I being the youngest. We were sensational! That was the only Follies in which I participated, but it gave me great experience and an abiding interest in the theatre which was revived at West Point in the 100th Nite Shows.

As a Junior and Senior in High School, I worked on the staff of the school newspaper, "The Campus Commentator." It was during these years that I got "the bug" to write poetry. Here are a few of the results of my efforts in this new undertaking:

"Spirit of The Pines"

Stately pines upon the campus,
Shafts of beauty buildéd high;
And for each a cherished mem'ry
From the happy days gone by.

In the hushed and peaceful twilight,
Looming high up in the air,
Comes a whisper, 'tis the echo
Of former students chatting there.

While the days go quickly forward
Taking each, his separate way,
'Twill always linger in our mem'ries
The stalwart pines of another day.

"The Herald of Thanksgiving"

When pumpkins turn from green to gold
And frost lies on the ground,
When fields of grain begin to blow
And corn stalks change to brown,
As evening suns begin to glow
And Autumn's trumpets sound,
'Tis The Herald of Thanksgiving.

The Churches filled with thankful folk
Who, with their voices, raise
A hymn of reverence and of joy;
A song of grateful praise
Resounds with music and with prayers
For guidance through the days,
'Tis The Herald of Thanksgiving.

"The Christmas Tree"

The Christmas Tree, with boughs all bent
From holding up each ornament,
Gives off a sparkle of good cheer,
To tell us that the morn is here,
When all the tots come charging down
From up the stairs and gather round
To see the toys Old Saint Nick
Has surely left: a ball to kick,
A drum to beat, a doll to dress,
A Teddy bear of friendliness.

But what has happened to The Tree?
The lights that were to shine for me
Have lost their glow and all their zest,
Because I lost my friendliness.

"The Heart of Night"

When the darkness of the evening is encirc'ling round about,
And the sun has gently closed another day,
When the twilight casts its shadows on a world of fear and doubt,

Then The Heart of Night begins its oft-tread way
Through the valley of decision, o'er the mountain of distress,
'Cross the creek of everlasting pain and death.
Though I stumble while I journey through this dark and gloomy path,
I press onward to the light of hope that's left.

When the mire of death is trampled and the lea of fear is crossed,
And the darkness of the night begins to clear;
Then a purple light appears through a mass of dripping moss,
As The Heart of Night is changed to something dear.

When the morning light is breaking and the weirdness of the night
Slowly changes into happiness and zest,
Then another night of sorrow is slowly passing by,
And the embers on the hearth are still, At Rest.

"Spring"

When the last snows of winter have melted and disappeared from the ground,
And the bareness of trees o'ercome with the budding of life –
When the robins and bluejays have turned to their home in the North –
'Tis signs of Spring – a new Spring.
A Spring that not only brings beauty of birds and beasts – and flowers
That fill the air with their fragrance,
But a Spring whose life contains happiness and hope for the lost,
Rest and sleep for the weary.

Spring – Happy Spring.

Also, while serving on the Staff of "The Campus Commentator", I was assigned to interview a few of the presentations of The Thomasville Entertainment Foundation. This was an organization conceived of and begun by Mrs. Emily Barkley Searcy (Mrs. William M., Jr.) in 1937 as the Thomasville Cooperative Concert Association. The performances were presented in the auditorium of the Municipal Building after it was completed in 1943. There were many outstanding presentations, some of which were of world renown and classic in quality. The one that I remember best was the Ballet Troupe of Mia Slavenska and her "premier danseur", George Zoritch. After the performance, with notebook in hand, I proceeded back stage to interview the principals. Miss Slavenska had a "splitting headache" and chose not to be interviewed, but Mr. Zoritch was kind to give me about thirty minutes of his time. While the other male dancers were busy getting dressed in one end of the men's room (the dressing rooms left a lot to be desired in those days), Mr. Zoritch and I sat in the other end and chatted about his career and about this, his first visit to the South. He had arrived early enough to have taken a tour of the downtown area, The Big Oak, and the Library. He paid the citizens of Thomasville many compliments on our town's hospitality. I thanked him for his time and wished him well, and I invited him back to our City whenever it would be possible. Mr. Zoritch later was associated with the Ballet Russe; and when he published his memoirs in 2000, I purchased a copy of <u>Ballet Mystique</u>, wrote to the author, and asked if he would inscribe my copy for my personal library. I reminded him of his visit to Thomasville and of our interview. I received a letter from the octogenarian agreeing to my request. When I sent the book to him and it was returned, the inscription was most cordial.

Attending the United States Military Academy at West Point, New York, was the best thing that could have happened to me at age eighteen. While my family had been engaged in every conflict in which the United States had been involved, from the American Revolution through World War II, I knew that I wanted to serve my Country in some fashion but didn't quite know how to go about it. As I have previously stated, one afternoon in my Senior Year in High School, I was called to the Plaza café to have a conversation with my Pastor, Brother Callaway; my father; and my Congressman, Judge Eugene Cox. It was Brother Callaway who stated that "we've decided that you should go to West Point."

Judge Cox said that if I passed my physical and mental tests, he would give me an appointment, which was and still is required for entry. The following February, I received a telegram "inviting" me to come to Fort Benning, Georgia, to take the required tests. I traveled from Thomasville to Columbus on the bus and arrived to find some four hundred young men awaiting the testing. For two days, we were x-rayed, poked, probed, looked at, queried, and shuffled back and forth within the hospital complex. On the third day, we were assembled in a large gymnasium and were given tests in English, Mathematics, Spatial Relations and Creative Writing. No results were given. We were told to go back home and wait patiently. I received no reports until the afternoon of my Baccalaureate Service on Sunday, the 30th of May, at about five PM, when a Western Union telegram arrived directing me to report to West Point on 1 July!

The Baccalaureate Service at The First Baptist Church was especially memorable for me, for I was invited by the organist, Mrs. Fleming, to be the guest organist for that service. I chose Mendelssohn's "War March of the Priests" as the Procession of the Senior Class, and as the Recessional, Luther's "A Mighty Fortress Is Our God." (During my High School years, I had competed in both the District and State Competitions in Piano and was awarded the top rating at the State level on four separate occasions.)

At the Graduation Ceremonies, held in The Municipal Auditorium on Friday, 4 June 1948, the Graduation Address was delivered by Mr. Robert Sherrod, a graduate of Thomasville High School in 1924 and a War Correspondent in World War II who wrote the book, <u>Tarawa</u>, and later the <u>History of Marine Corps Aviation in World War II</u>. Robert was the son of one of my father's sixty first cousins. During the awarding of Medals and Prizes, I had the honor to receive the First Robert Sherrod Award for Journalism. As I reflect on my High School years, I am reminded how prophetic was the selection of our Class Motto: "We Shall Make Footprints on The Sands of Time." So many members of our Class of 1948 have achieved great honors and awards. I have always been proud to have been a part of this great Class.

📖 📖 📖

My four years at West Point were challenging and interesting, and both happy and sad. The education was superb. The physical training was demanding, but results were immediate and obvious. Plebe, or Fourth Class, Year was like any other training at any other military institution, only harder and more intense. Throughout the year, I tried to find some humor wherever it could be located, to ameliorate the intensity of being "the lowest form of humanity." I remember one particular day, just before we formed up for lunch, one of my roommates had told us a humorous story. It was particularly funny and I could not stop laughing, even after I arrived in formation, bracing as only a Plebe could do. One of the upperclassmen in our Company came up to my face, almost nose-to-nose, and said, "Mr. Raiford, repeat after me: I am a laughing idiot." Well, I thought, this is too good to be true. I replied: "Sir, you are a laughing idiot." The proverbial roof fell in. On my person converged several more upperclassmen who felt I needed extra instruction. What made it bearable was the fact that I enjoyed the humor of it all.

Another memorable event in my Plebe Year was the January, 1949, rail trip from West Point to Washington, DC, to march in President Harry Truman's Inauguration Day Parade. While the day was cold, the weather was clear. Since the West Point Corps of Cadets always by tradition leads the Inaugural Parade, we had passed the Reviewing Stand and were at the "decompression" area by about 1430 hours (that's 2:30 in the afternoon for all you civilian readers). The Corps was not scheduled to form up at the rail yard until 2200 hours (10 PM) for our trip back to the Academy. So we Cadets had several hours to enjoy the City of Washington. However, most everything was closed for the day except the restaurants and bars. Having heard glowing reports about a place down on the waterfront called The New England Raw Bar, several of us decided to check it out. We were all still in our uniforms, so being on our best behavior was a given. The Bar, hanging out over the water of the Tidal Basin, had a wooden floor, the planks of which were not quite fitted, so that one could view the water while sitting on the barstool. After we had had a few rounds of beer and partaken of some of the delicious seafood, we decided to remain there before returning to the train. So we did, for about six hours! I don't remember if there was a prize awarded, but I do remember that I ate the most Cherrystone Clams in our group! All of us arrived safely back at the train at the appointed hour, with grins on our faces, happy as a clam!

During my Plebe Year, I was required to memorize much material, "to improve my mind." Some of it was pure doggerel, such as the following:

"If the fresh skin of an animal, cleaned and divested of all hair, fat and other extraneous matter, be immersed in a dilute solution of tannic acid, a chemical combination ensues; the gelatinous tissue is converted into a non-putrescible substance, impervious to, and insoluble in, water; this sir, is leather."

Notwithstanding, the most important item of my memory work was "The Cadet Prayer":

"O God, our Father, Thou Searcher of Men's hearts, help us to draw near to Thee in sincerity and truth. May our religion be filled with gladness and may our worship of Thee be natural. Strengthen and increase our admiration for honest dealing and clean thinking, and suffer not our hatred of hypocrisy and pretense ever to diminish. Encourage us to live above the common level of life. Make us to choose the harder right instead of the easier wrong, and never to be content with the half truth when the whole can be won. Endow us with courage that is born of loyalty to all that is noble and worthy, that scorns to compromise with vice and injustice and knows no fear when truth and right are in jeopardy. Guard us against flippancy and irreverence in the scared things of life.

Grant us new ties of friendship and new opportunities of service. Kindle our hearts in fellowship with those of a cheerful countenance, and soften our hearts with sympathy for those who sorrow and suffer. Help us to maintain the honor of the Corps untarnished and unsullied and to show forth in our lives the ideals of West Point in doing our duty to Thee and to our Country. All of which we ask in the name of the Great Friend and Master of men. Amen."

The motto of the Academy is "Duty, Honor, Country." It was General Robert E. Lee who said that "Duty" was the most important word in the English language. "We should do our Duty in all things. We can do nothing less."

A few additional items of wisdom I was taught included the following:

"Don't act important. If you are important, everybody will know it. If you are not, you can't convince anyone that you are." My father had a great paraphrase of this: "If you have to tell people who you are, you aren't."

"If you look over your shoulder and have a following, you are a leader; if you don't have a following, you are probably not a leader and certainly not a politician." Again my father had a great paraphrase: "Sometimes you have to tell a man to go to Hell, but make him look forward to the trip."

"If you want to control others, control yourself first."

"Learn how and when to delegate authority and responsibility."

"One of the best ways to demonstrate loyalty is to learn to take blame and give credit."

In April of 1951, I was in New York City on business for the Academy and happened to walk by the 57th Street showroom of the Carl Fischer, Inc. music store. Displayed in their window was the new sheet music of the song made famous by General Douglas MacArthur in his recent address to the Congress of the United States, in which he closed his remarks with the statement "old soldiers never die, they just pass away." I went into the store and purchased a copy. I was dressed in my Cadet uniform. The next week, I received a letter from the Corporate Offices of the Carl Fischer Music Company stating in part, "It was a great pleasure and satisfaction to us to hear that a West Point Cadet had bought the very first copy of our new vocal arrangement of 'Old Soldiers Never Die'." The letter is signed by Marcia M. Connor, Director of Public Relations for the firm.

In later years, I was able to get General MacArthur to autograph my copy of the "sleeve" containing the RCA LP recording of the speech he delivered at West Point on 12 May 1962, entitled "Duty, Honor, Country", the motto of West Point.

In the Fall of my First Class Year, one of my classmates was invited by a former girlfriend, who then lived in Greenwich, Connecticut, to be one of her escorts at her forthcoming debutante party. She also asked him to bring along one of his classmates. So I was invited to accompany him. The two of us, along with two guys from Harvard and two guys from Princeton, were to comprise her "squad of escorts." On the appointed Saturday, after the usual SAMI (Saturday Morning Inspection), he and I departed the Academy on one of our authorized Senior Weekends.

Since the evening affair in Greenwich was formal, we decided to wear our "formal" uniforms, brass buttons and all. Having no transportation to get to Greenwich, we took a taxi from Highland Falls, the small village at the southern exit of the Academy grounds, to the Bear Mountain Bridge, about six miles southward. There we were able to "hitch" a ride eastward to the Taconic State Parkway, where we caught a ride going south in a hearse which was returning from a funeral upstate. Since we did not want to "crease" our trousers any further than necessary, and to make a noteworthy arrival at our destination, we lay in the back of the hearse, having already persuaded the driver to "deliver" us to the Greenwich Country Club. You can imagine the "entrance" we made when a hearse pulled up in front of the Club, amongst all the limousines and "black ties." Quite frankly, I don't think the debutante of the evening had a chance at the spotlight!

The next time I saw President Truman was on 20 May 1952, the day of the West Point Convocation. As a planned event of The Sesquicentennial Celebration (my Class of 1952 was the 150th Class to graduate from the Academy), all the Institutions of Higher Learning throughout the world had been invited to send a representative to the Academy to celebrate West Point as an Institute of Superlative Academic Achievement. Several hundred Institutions throughout the world sent representatives, each wearing the robe and colored cowl of that Institution. The Convocation Parade was led by the Chairman of the Joint Chiefs of Staff, General of the Army Omar N. Bradley, a graduate of West Point's Class of 1915, carrying the Mace of Academic Authority; followed by The

President of the United States; and then the academic representatives in order of the founding of their Institutions, led by the University of Bologna, Italy, founded in 1036. Of course, the weather did not cooperate; and because of the torrential rain, the entire procession marched in the cavernous Field House.

Another highlight of my four years at West Point took place in the Fall of 1951. I was a member of the Cadet Chapel Choir and had come to admire and respect the organist, Mr. Frederic C. Meyer, who had come to that position in 1911, one year after the Chapel had been constructed. It was Mr. Meyer who had shepherded the design and installation of the pipe organ. The original organ contained 2,406 pipes. During my years at the Academy, the organ had been expanded to some 15,500 individual pipes and was still growing. It is now the largest church organ in the world, containing over 23,000 individual pipes. Just a few days before Thanksgiving that year, Mr. Meyer telephoned me in my barracks and asked if I would play the Thanksgiving Service for him, since his sister in Ohio was not well and he planned to drive out to spend the holidays with her. I had never even sat on the organ bench, but Mr. Meyer knew of my musical talents and had asked me to play piano for several individual and group rehearsals. When I accepted his offer contingent upon receiving the approval of the Superintendent, Mr. Meyer informed me that the Superintendent had already approved his request and, in addition, I was to meet him that evening at the organ to rehearse the entire Service. Mr. Meyer informed me that I was the only Cadet to have played the organ up until that time, and the official records at the Academy do not indicate any subsequent Cadet being so honored. I am pleased to note that the Service went as scheduled, the Cadet Choir marched in four-abreast as usual, and my fears before the Service were quickly extinguished when

I realized that I had been placed in charge of the whole "shebang"! That is what "leadership training" is all about.

On another rather memorable occasion, 19 January 1952, during the Sesquicentennial Celebrations, the Academy was holding a Ceremony for the unveiling of a portrait of General Robert E. Lee, a former Superintendent of West Point and a graduate of the Class of 1829. I decided to honor the General by wearing a Confederate hat with my cadet uniform! After all, it was his birthday. Needless to say, the Officer of the Day stopped me on my way to my first class of the day and "wrote me up" for being out of uniform. This was a very serious offense and called for an appearance before the Tactical Regimental Commander, Lieutenant Colonel Jefferson J. Irving, who was from Louisiana. When I explained to Colonel Irving that I, as a fellow Southerner, meant no disrespect to the uniform but was only trying to show respect to General Lee on his birthday; I was given the minimum, only five demerits rather than the usual punishment tours, "walking the area" with a rifle. To jump forward a few years, after the War in Korea had ended, I was selected to be the Aide-de-Camp to the Commanding General of the 45th Infantry Division. On one occasion I was sent to Tokyo and appeared at the office of now Major General Jefferson J. Irving. As I entered and saluted, the General said, "Well, Raiford, what are you up for this time?"

During my years at the Academy, I participated in several sports but concentrated on the high hurdles in track. Three of my close fellow track friends were Buzz Aldrin, who was one year ahead of me, and my classmates, Ed White and Mike Collins, all three of whom became Astronauts. I chose not to fly! Other activities in which I engaged included the Russian Language Club, the Handball Club, the Chapel Choir, The Chapel Chimers, the Dialectic Society, the Glee Club and the 100th Night Show. The latter is a stage revue, written, directed, and acted in by Cadets on the weekend of the 100th Night before that year's graduation date. I wrote music and sometimes the lyrics for three successive shows. In my Senior Year, I wrote all the music and some of the lyrics for the Show, called "Ah-Men!". It was such a hit that we were allowed three performances rather than the usual two. In addition, the singer, Eddie Fisher, then a Corporal in the U.S. Army stationed in New Jersey, was detailed temporarily to West Point to assist us in the production.

The Chapel Chimers was a select group of men who not only had a musical talent but also had the brawn to exhibit it on the Chapel Chimes. The Chimes were located in the tower above the Cadet Chapel. To get to them, one had to ascend the stairs at the front of the Chapel to the top-most level, then go through a small door and proceed along the rafters to that point above the crossing of the Chapel. Then one had to crawl up a few more steps and stop on a platform directly below the tower containing all the different-toned bells. Each of the huge bells was attached to a long cord which was attached to a wooden handle which was levered from a fulcrum. To ring a particular bell, the chimer would push down on the lever with "a mighty force." The Chimer Squad was composed of eight men who took turns, on a rotational basis, to ring the chimes fifteen minutes before the evening meal in the Mess Hall. Usually played were the Westminster, Traditional and Anglican sets of notes, but occasionally other tunes emerged. On a particular challenge from my Kentucky roommate (who later was an Usher in my wedding), I played "My Old Kentucky Home." The comments in the Mess Hall that evening ranged from "great" to "just wait; you'll hear about that!" No repercussions ensued.

On one occasion just prior to the Christmas break, the West Point Glee Club, composed of some one hundred, sixty male voices traveled to New York City and combined with the almost four hundred female voices of Hunter College and performed Handel's "Hallelujah" Chorus, accompanied by two grand pianos, an organ, and a twenty-two piece orchestra. It was a magnificent performance!

Another incident in my Cadet musical career was most memorable. As the Chairman of West Point's Special Programs Committee in my Senior Year, it was my duty (and my pleasure) to travel to New York City and meet with the various Concert Bureaus and try to arrange for individual and groups of artists to come to the Academy on Sunday evenings for the entertainment of the Corps of Cadets. On one particular Saturday, after I had completed my assigned duties and had the evening free, I went downtown to a restaurant called Asti's, at 13 East 12th Street. Asti's was world famous in the 1940s, -50s and -60s, as the place where the waiters, the hatcheck girl, and the bartenders all sang grand opera. On this particular evening, when I arrived, dressed in my Cadet tunic, the piano player, whom I had known from other venues, was seated, as usual, at the Steinway grand in the center of the restaurant. The top had been removed so the volume from the piano could be better heard throughout the room. As I greeted him, Roger said "Take over, I need a break." The time was about 2300 hours. As I began to play, the requests came in, and I was able to comply with most of them. When the group sang "The Anvil Chorus" from the opera, "La Traviata", the bartenders would ring the cash registers, right on cue! At about midnight, a lady entered the front door and was immediately recognized by everyone, except me. She draped herself in the crook of the piano and asked, "Where's Roger?" When told that he was on break and that I would be happy to accompany her, she indicated the aria she had chosen, one that

I had heard many times but had never seen the score. The Lord gave me a talent to "play by ear" when it was called for. This was one of those times. As I played the introduction, the singer looked at me curiously. As she began to sing, she continued to look at me because she knew I was "faking it." As she opened her mouth, I immediately recognized the voice of Kirsten Flagstad, the great Metropolitan Opera soprano who, at that time, was one of the world's greatest singers. We made it through the aria and she accepted the wild applause from her many admirers in the restaurant. As I stood, I reached for her hand, gave it a kiss, and said

"Thank you, Madam."

"Oh, no," she replied, "I thank you. That was an experience."

The West Point Glee Club has a long history of singing at Army Hospitals around the Nation and on television. During my Senior Year, we performed on "The Kate Smith Hour", "The Tallulah Bankhead Show", and multiple appearances on "The Ed Sullivan Show." On 22 February 1952, during the NBC Television show, "The Kate Smith Hour", as the Cadet Director of the West Point Glee Club, I had the honor to present to Miss Smith a brochure on the forthcoming Sesquicentennial Celebrations of the Academy and to engage her in conversation. Supported by the Glee Club, Miss Smith sang Irving Berlin's "God Bless America." I have a copy of this television show on tape in my personal film library. The Glee Club also made a recording of West Point songs for Columbia Records; and on the 5th of January, 1952, the Glee Club and the West Point Army

Band gave a joint concert in Carnegie Hall in New York City. I had the honor of being the accompanist and the Cadet Director that year and was honored to play piano during that concert. In the preceding December, I was driven by an Academy driver to Albany, New York, to the Office of the Governor, Thomas E. Dewey, to deliver to him two tickets to the forthcoming Carnegie Hall Concert. In the picture of the two of us which hangs on my "I like me" wall, Governor Dewey appears to be much shorter than I, who stands 6'3". In fact, Governor Dewey is standing on a box, not visible in the picture, for he was only about 5' tall.

Prior to the January concert, I wrote a letter to Mrs. Ethel Dekle Silva, who had been my piano teacher in Thomasville, informing her that I was going to play in Carnegie Hall. (Mrs. Silva, the widow of Thomas J. Silva, a cotton broker who lost his life on the Lusitania in 1915, had graduated from Wesleyan Conservatory in Macon, Georgia, in 1907. She was a classmate of Ching-ling Soong, who later became Madam Sun Yat-Sen. Mrs. Silva's grandfather, John W. Dekle, was the first white child born in Thomas County, Georgia, after its creation in 1825.) Mrs. Silva wrote back that she didn't know if I was "ready" for Carnegie Hall and that she was coming to New York to audition me! She traveled from Thomasville to New York City on the trains. I got permission from the Superintendent of West Point to meet Mrs. Silva in New York City for the "audition." When I finished playing, Mrs. Silva, with tears in her eyes, said that she had never before had a pupil play in Carnegie Hall, but that she believed I was "ready." I felt that she was really proud of her former pupil.

Graduation was on 3 June 1952. I was commissioned a Second Lieutenant in the Army Corps of Engineers. Even though they had been divorced in 1950, my parents, still friends, came to West Point for my Graduation.

Accompanying them were my mother's oldest sister, Mrs. Russell May (Aunt D); and my father's only sister, Mrs. Scott Walker (Aunt T); and my sister and her husband, Francis Brannon, and their daughter, Margaret. The speaker at my graduation was The Honorable Thomas K. Finletter, Secretary of the Air Force. As I stepped off the platform after receiving my diploma, I approached my father and we saluted each other. (My father had been a private in World War I.) As we embraced, with tears in his eyes, he whispered in my ear, "I now know what I have lived my entire life for."

Five days after my graduation from West Point, I had the honor of addressing the Key Club International Convention at the Stevens Hotel in Chicago, Illinois. In attendance were about eight thousand young men from all over America. My assigned topic was "Leadership." Even though I had been commissioned less than a week, the leaders of Key Club International thought I, as a former Key Clubber in Thomasville, was qualified to present myself to the assemblage as an "authority." I made many friends during that meeting who have remained close acquaintances over the years.

My first Army assignment was Fort Belvoir, Virginia, for eight more weeks of basic engineering training! Then to Fort Leonard Wood, Missouri, for more training in the Combat Arms before going to Korea. Fort Leonard Wood was, at that time, a most desolate place. In fact, the commentator, Walter Winchell, on one of his Sunday night radio broadcasts, said: "Mr. and Mrs. America: If your son is in Korea, write to him. If he is at Leonard Wood, pray for him!" After a thirty day leave back in Georgia, I and about twenty of my West Point classmates, all Engineers, sailed from Seattle, Washington, aboard the U.S. Naval Ship Marine Lynx, in March, arriving at Inchon, Korea, on Easter Sunday morning, 5 April 1953. (Accompanying us on that voyage was Captain George S. Patton, III, who had graduated from the Academy on D-Day, 6 June 1944, and with whom I later served on the Board of Trustees of the Association of Graduates of West Point. George married the older sister of a young lady that I later dated in Washington, DC.)

After processing and attending an Easter Service, and spending one night in Uijongbu, near Inchon, I arrived at my unit, Charlie Company (Company C), 120th Engineer Combat Battalion, 45th Infantry Division, located near the western slope of "Heartbreak Ridge." There were four other Officers in Charlie Company at that time. As a Platoon Leader, it was my duty to maintain the combat readiness of the troops under my command, as well as their morale. The latter was by far the more difficult. Charlie Company had several Battalion-assigned duties: We had to maintain the roads in the rear of the front lines, by operating the gravel-crushing machines and the asphalt plant; we erected and maintained two tramways to the crest of Heartbreak Ridge so that the troops could receive their daily food rations and their ammunition; and I had to make several trips to the "Ridge" to report to the Commanding Officer of the Regiment my Company was supporting. During the period from my arrival in Charlie Company up until 3 June, one year to the day after graduating from West Point, I continued to perform all duties assigned to me by the Company Commander. But by this time, the other four Officers had either rotated home or had been assigned to other duties within the Battalion. On that date, 3 June, I was given command of Charlie Company, although I was not promoted to First Lieutenant until about a month later, on 29 June. From then until the War ended on 27 July, we remained in the vicinity of "Heartbreak Ridge." On that day, 3 June, I gathered my six West Point classmates who were in the area and we dined in the trenches on "Heartbreak Ridge" on canned rock lobster (compliments of my father's grocery store) and champagne from the PX (45th Division Post Exchange), which we cooled in the waters of the Mundung-ni River, which ran north to south just west of "Heartbreak Ridge."

At the cessation of hostilities, our Engineer Battalion was assigned the responsibility of erecting a barbed-wire fence, two hundred feet from the battle line at the end of the war, across the entire front of the 45th Division. Each of us Company Commanders within the Battalion was apportioned a part of the task, which, in my case, was delegated to the one hundred, twenty men in my Company. As the only Officer in the Company, I supervised the construction of that fence on a daily basis until the task was completed.

At the conclusion of hostilities, I was awarded the Bronze Star Medal, and every member of the 45th Infantry Division was awarded the Korean Presidential Unit Citation by President Syngman Rhee.

In later years, it was my pleasure to know, and call my friend, Colonel Russell P. "Red" Reeder, Jr., West Point Class of 1926, who was the originator of The Bronze Star Medal for the United States Army. In my collection of memorabilia, I have a monograph detailing the origin and official recognition of the creation of this medal, inscribed to me by Colonel Reeder.

After the cessation of hostilities, our Division was moved off the MLR (Main Line of Resistance), back to a reserve area in the vicinity of a small village called Inje in the Yang-gu Valley. After we had gotten settled in, several men in my Company and others from the rest of the Battalion, pooled their resources and ordered, with my approval, from the Sears catalog a large water pump. In the village of Inje, there was, in the village center, a large wooden trough which was filled with water each morning by the women of the village who took their water jugs to the Hwachon Reservoir, about three miles northward. The men in Charlie Company thought it would be a nice gesture of humanitarianism to build a windmill in the village and erect the pump therein, so the women would not have to make the daily trek to the Reservoir. The windmill was erected, the well was dug, and, after the pump arrived from Sears, it was installed and put into operation. Upon completion of the work, I met with the Mayor of the village and suggested that we have a brief ceremony dedicating the windmill and pump, as a gift from the Engineers of the 45th Division. The Mayor agreed, and the next morning, the townspeople gathered around the windmill as I spoke, with an interpreter, and formally presented the new "source of water" to the village. The thanks of the mayor were polite, but I noticed that the women of the town were silent and unsmiling. The next morning, we Engineers visited "our work" to see how things were going. The windmill had been taken down and the pump was nowhere to be found. When I asked the Mayor what had happened, he was most apologetic and explained to me that, by having the water pumped in the village square, we were depriving the women of their time away from their husbands and families and the only time they had to visit with the other women of the village. The women of Korea had been doing this for thousands of years, the Mayor explained. He further added, "Why are you Americans always trying to change the ways of others to be like yourselves?" My solemn wish that morning was that we Americans would benefit from this experience and be more tolerant of the ways, customs and religions of the rest of the world before we undertake to change them.

Shortly after this incident, I received a call from the G-1 (Chief of Personnel) at the 45th Division Headquarters, informing me that I had been invited to be interviewed for the position of Aide-de-Camp to the Commanding General, Major General Paul D. Harkins, West Point Class of 1929. At the completion of the interview and after I had been offered the position, I asked General Harkins how he had selected me. He stated that he had looked through the entire list of First Lieutenants in the Division, and that my name was the only one he recognized, since I had been Director of the Glee Club when he had been Commandant of Cadets. This is the only time in my years of service to my country that I was selected for a position or an assignment based on my musical abilities!

Subsequent to my becoming the General's Aide, on one of my visits to Seoul, I witnessed a procession of nuns on their way to the Myongdong Cathedral. They were chanting in a monotone, the theme of which fascinated me. I sat down on the curb, pulled out a piece of paper, and scribbled some notes for a yet-to-be-written tone poem. After returning to the States, I completed what became known as "The Cathedral at Seoul." In later years, during the week of the Dedication of the Korean War Memorial in Washington, DC, I was asked to play my composition in the National Cathedral, on a Steinway grand piano in the Crossing of the Cathedral. I have also played it in concert in 1991 in Seoul, Korea; for President Jimmy Carter and guests in Washington; and twice again in the National Cathedral.

On several occasions, General Harkins and I flew down to Seoul by helicopter to be the guests at dinner of President and Mrs. Rhee. General Harkins had known the Rhees when he was Chief of Staff of the 8th United States Army, Headquartered in Seoul. Mrs. Rhee was Viennese and spoke very good English. Many years later, in September 1991, I re-visited Korea and paid a social call on Mrs. Rhee. She was then in her nineties but quite lucid in her recollection of our previous visits. On my departure, she gave me an inscribed pictorial book on the life of President Rhee.

After I had been the General's Aide for a few weeks, he asked me if I still had any "pull" with my Engineers. It was his desire to have the Engineers design and build a handball court in the Yang-gu Valley. General Harkins had been an active handball player when he was the Commandant of Cadets at West Point; and during my four years at the Academy, I had taken up the sport in the off-seasons from track. After the standard-sized, six-wall court was completed, which included an area beneath it for a grate and a blower to keep the court heated in the winter months; the General and I partnered with several other Officers in the Headquarters Staff. On several occasions, General Taylor and his Aide "choppered" up from Seoul to challenge General Harkins and me. It also was a good opportunity to get to know General Taylor better.

During the Fall of 1953, I was eligible for R&R (a one-week leave from duty called Rest and Recuperation). I chose to go to Tokyo, Japan. My other choices were Hong Kong and Singapore. Although I did not go to Hong Kong, I reviewed the catalog of a friend, detailing the clothes that could be "special ordered" from there. I sent my measurements and my personal check for $25.00 for a custom tailored white cashmere dinner jacket which arrived in Korea in just three weeks. The fit was superb!

After the orders were published (Standard Operating Procedure) and distribution was made throughout the Far East Command (by Order of the Commanding General of the Armed Forces Far East Command [AFFE], General Mark W. Clark), I received a telegram from AFFE Headquarters informing me that I had been invited to spend my R&R as the guest of General and Mrs. Clark at their Quarters in Tokyo. I had known the Clarks when he was in Command at Fortress Monroe, Virginia, while I was a Cadet at West Point. I had also double-dated with their daughter and had spent time at their Quarters at Monroe. An invitation of this magnitude posed grave problems for a First Lieutenant. In one sense, this was a Command Performance; in another, it was a high honor; and in a third, I didn't know if my visit to Tokyo would be curtailed in the activities I had planned. Thinking solely of my career, I accepted the invitation and when our plane arrived in Tokyo, the General's staff car and driver awaited me at the airport. (Later, back in Korea, this required much explanation among my fellow travelers.) The driver deposited me in front of the General's Quarters, a huge mansion of undetermined vintage which the Japanese had offered to him. The General and Mrs. Clark greeted me on the veranda and discussed with me some of the events they had already planned for me, to include a dinner that evening at the residence of the Mayor of Tokyo. When I, who was dressed in my khaki uniform, informed the General that I did not have any civilian clothes with me, he said for me not to worry. Knowing that he and I were the same height and approximate weight, he had had laid out on my bed, a suit and a shirt and tie, with a pair of black dress shoes and socks under the bed. The evening went well –- I was overwhelmed, as only a twenty-three year old First Lieutenant from Georgia, in the company of the Commanding General of all Military Forces in the Far East, could have been. When we returned to their

Quarters, Mrs. Clark asked me to play some selections on their grand piano. (I had done so at Fortress Monroe.) Before we all retired for the evening, the General asked me if I would like to do a little putting in the morning. (There was a putting green in front of the mansion.) Having had instructions in golf at West Point, but having had little time to practice since Graduation, I accepted the General's offer. I was instructed to meet the General on the green at 0530 hours. In some locations, this is called "oh-dark-thirty." When I arrived promptly at 0530 in clothes also provided by my host, I noticed that the General wore white shorts with four stars embroidered on one leg! Later that morning, the General indicated that he knew I might like to spend some time in downtown Tokyo by myself, so I was taken to a subway stop, given a map, and sent on my way. I spent the day shopping at the Matsuzukaya Department Store on The Ginza and at Mikimoto's main pearl shop in the arcade under the Imperial Hotel. That evening I went to a ballet performance of "Swan Lake" in Hibiya Park and the next evening to a performance of the Kabuki. Since the Kabuki is a continuous telling of Japanese history, one can go in and come out of the performance at any time. It was fascinating. I had dinner one evening at Suihiro's, probably one of the all-time great Japanese restaurants. On another evening, with one of my fellow travelers from Korea, we took a pedicab from downtown Tokyo to a restaurant on the outskirts of the city, known for its music as well as its cuisine. As we walked in, we were greeted by the proprietor, a blind Japanese gentleman of an indeterminate age, who spoke some English. After we had been seated and served sake and orange cakes, the proprietor asked me if I had any requests of classical music. On the wall behind his "cage" were racks from floor to ceiling, running the entire length of the restaurant, of ten- and twelve-inch red-seal records, mostly of classical arias, I was told. Trying to show some "couth" as well as a musical education, I requested one of my favorite arias, the tenor duet from Georges Bizet's "The Pearl Fishers." Running his hand along one row of the records, the blind man pulled the requested record, recorded by Caruso and Scotti, and put it on the old Victrola. My friend and I spent several hours eating, drinking and listening to beautiful music. It was an exceptionally pleasant evening.

In later years, I received a letter from General Clark, when he was the President of The Citadel in Charleston, South Carolina, which said in part, "Mrs. Clark and I well remember your short visit with us in Tokyo and how you played the piano so beautifully." As an accompaniment to this letter, a copy of his book, From the Danube to the Yalu, was enclosed, with the inscription "With deep appreciation of your splendid service with me in the Far East. Mark W. Clark."

I remained with General Harkins as his Aide-de-Camp until the 45th Infantry Division was selected to be the first Infantry Division to return to the States from Korea. General Harkins transferred command of the Division to Brigadier General Harvey J. Fischer who returned to the States with the 45th Division Troops, while General Harkins became Commanding General of the 24th Infantry Division and asked me to continue as his Aide-de-Camp.

During the Christmas season of 1953, two events occurred which were most pleasant and memorable. A United Service Organization (USO) Show arrived in the Yang-gu Valley. The featured person therein was Miss Marilyn Monroe. At the same time, The Vicar of the United States Army, Francis Joseph Cardinal Spellman, arrived in the Valley to say a Christmas Eve Mass. Of course, both were invited to dine in the General's Mess for the Christmas Eve dinner. As the Aide-de-Camp, it was my duty to prepare the seating list for the occasion. All members of the General Staff, plus the Commanders of the major units within the 45th Division, were invited to dine. When I presented to General Harkins the proposed seating arrangement, he noted that I had put the Cardinal on his right and Miss Monroe on his left. He did not question my reasoning, but commented with approbation that "your mother obviously brought you up right." As an aside, I should note that the father of General Harkins was, for many years, the Society Editor of the "Boston Globe." (For you readers who may not be familiar with military protocol, military ranks usually take precedence over civilians. The title, "Vicar of the United States Army" is considered a military rank and even outranks any "civilian" lady present.)

General Harkins and I celebrated our birthdays together in the month of May. During May of 1954, another USO Show appeared in the Yang-gu Valley, this one featured Miss Debbie Reynolds, who was accompanied by her mother and Miss Susan Zanuck, the daughter of Mr. Darryl Zanuck, the Hollywood producer. At dinner in the General's Mess, two birthday cakes had been prepared by the General's Mess Sergeant. The General asked the mother of Miss Reynolds to assist him in cutting his cake, and I asked Miss Reynolds to assist me with mine. Coincidentally, Miss Reynolds was, at that time, dating Mr. Eddie Fisher, who had assisted us at West Point two years before in the preparation of our 100th Nite Show. Small world; great conversation!

Just before the departure of the 45th Division from Korea, General Harkins indicated that he would like to host a dinner for all General Officers in the United Nations Command in Korea, plus the President of Korea. As the General's Aide-de-Camp, the duty fell to me to set up the dinner. General Harkins further stated that he would like each General Officer seated in order of his date of rank. I got on the horn (telephone) and extended the invitation to each of the United Nations Commands in Korea, obtaining the full name, rank and date of rank of each General Officer. Name cards were made by the 45th Division Headquarters staff and the dinner proceeded as scheduled. However, at the last minute, even while the attendees were filing into the mess hall; I, and several other 1st Lieutenants who I had asked to assist me, were re-arranging the name cards due to the no-shows. What made this so difficult is the fact that the order of rank alternates from the right to the left of the Host. When everyone had been seated, I was able to breathe a sigh of relief and catch the eye of General Harkins who indicated, with a wink, his pleasure with the results of the late-hour pandemonium. Once again, I realized that I was experiencing "agonies of enjoyment."

At the conclusion of the dinner, General Harkins introduced General Maxwell D. Taylor, Commanding General of the Eighth Army, under whose command were included all military personnel of all Nations serving under the United Nations in Korea. General Taylor arose, acknowledged President Rhee, and proceeded to deliver his remarks, in Korean! No one present knew that General Taylor had been studying the Korean language during his lunch hours for several months. Being the linguist that he was, his remarks were not only impeccably delivered but also warmly received by President Rhee and all the Korean General Officers present. At the conclusion of General Taylor's remarks, Mr. Rhee rose, and with great emotion in his voice and on his face, thanked General Taylor, in English, for the honor paid to the Korean people by delivering his remarks in their language, considered by most linguists to be exceedingly difficult to perfect.

For services rendered during my two assignment as Aides-de-Camp to General Harkins, I was awarded two Army Commendation Medals.

I remained with General Harkins from the late summer of 1953 until we departed for the States in the summer of 1954. On the day we left Inje in the Yang-gu Valley, we flew by helicopter to Seoul and departed, in a propellor-driven aircraft, about two in the morning, after having a breakfast of bacon and eggs, toast and coffee. We landed in Tokyo in time for a breakfast of bacon and eggs and toast and coffee. We then departed for Midway Island and arrived in time for a late breakfast of bacon and eggs and toast and coffee. When we departed Midway, the General opined that he hoped our next meal would be different. Upon arrival in Hawaii, a brunch was served. You guessed it: bacon and eggs and toast and coffee! We remained in Hawaii as the guest of General Clark Ruffner, Commanding General of the Pacific Theater. General Harkins mused that he hoped the efficient refueling of our plane would not prohibit his visit to the beaches. We both were quite pleased that it took three full days to refuel the plane!

We finally left Hawaii bound for the States. We landed at an Air Force base outside the San Francisco Bay area. It was here that General Harkins and I separated. He was destined for duty in the Pentagon in Washington, DC, and I had some accumulated leave time before reporting to my next assignment: River and Harbor Duty with the Corps of Engineers in Nashville, Tennessee. I proceeded to my home in South Georgia by way of a most involved route: I caught a military flight from California to Dallas, Texas, then another from Dallas to Fort Benning, Georgia. From there I got another flight to Panama City, Florida, where I was able to get a bus to Tallahassee, Florida. These combined flights only took two days. My sister and brother-in-law met me in Tallahassee and we drove to their home in Cairo (pronounced "Kay-row"), Georgia, where I rested for several days before visiting friends and relatives. My parents had divorced in 1950 while I was at West Point, after more than thirty-two years of marriage. Each was living in Thomasville, only 14 miles from Cairo. After a few weeks in South Georgia, visiting with each of my parents and friends, I drove to Nashville, Tennessee, having purchased a Chevrolet from my brother-in-law, who was a used car dealer. It was not the car I really wanted but it was "wheels" and in my price bracket.

I reported in to the Nashville, Tennessee, District Headquarters of the Ohio River Division of the U.S. Army Corps of Engineers and was assigned as one of two Assistants to the District Engineer, Colonel Gilbert Dorland, West Point Class of 1936. The other Assistant was my West Point classmate, Max Howard. Our duties consisted of working with the civilian staff engaged in the construction of both the Old Hickory and the Cheatham Powerhouses and Dams on the Cumberland River, both outside of Nashville. While the job was interesting and educational, I found it somewhat difficult to offer suggestions to men who had been in this business longer than I had been alive. I can truthfully say that the year spent there on construction projects taught me quite a bit about dealing with people over whom I had responsibility and authority, but to whom I was constantly looking for guidance and instruction.

As soon as I got settled in Nashville, I determined that the Chevrolet had to go. My image was being damaged. So I was able to negotiate a trade-in for a new Oldsmobile Super 88 Holiday Coupe, green and white, with white sidewalls. As a twenty-four year old First Lieutenant in the United States Army, living in a major metropolitan area, in a basement apartment in a private home, and driving a brand new Olds Super 88, I was quite the "cat." I had recently begun to date the daughter of one of the premier trial lawyers in the United States and had been introduced to "Nashville Society" at several dinners and dances at the Belle Meade Country Club. Life was good and I was enjoying it immensely.

On one particular evening when I visited the Nashville Night Club called "Blues Alley", the piano player, a recent friend, asked if I would take over for a while. As I did, a young Air Force Corporal in uniform stepped up to the piano and asked me if I read music. When I said that I did, he put a hand-written score in front of me and we presented, for the first time, an original composition, "Honeycomb." The singer was Jimmie Rodgers. We played and sang together often that Fall.

At the dedication of the Cheatham Dam and Powerhouse, Mr. Owen Cheatham and his two daughters were the guests of honor. Max and I were "detailed" to escort the two young ladies while they were in Nashville. At that time, Mr. Cheatham was the Chairman of the Board of the Georgia-Pacific Corporation. At the following Thanksgiving, I was invited to fly to New York and join the family for dinner at their home in Manhattan. This I did. It was also a chance to get to know the older of the two daughters a little better and to conclude, after that long weekend, that I did not "fit" in their idea of "society."

Then came Christmastime, 1954. I drove to Thomasville for the holidays during which time I was invited to go to the Kappa Alpha Fraternity Dance at the Glen Arven Country Club on Christmas Eve, as an "extra." (The Glen Arven Country Club and Golf Course are the second oldest in the State of Georgia, having been built in 1892.) The gentleman, with whom I went to the dance, and I decided that we would go "snaking." This is a term which indicates that a male is attending alone with the intent of going home with another's date. However, fate intervened.

Mrs. Homer Hecker Berger had moved back to Thomasville from Kansas City, Missouri, after the death of her husband in 1950. She had designed and built a new home on the Old Monticello Road, just outside the city limit. After living there a few months, she decided that it was "too remote" for a widow and that she would be more comfortable in the city proper. So she designed and built a second house at 102 Springdale Circle, at the intersection with East Clay Street. It was at this Christmas Season that her daughter, Mary Chase, who was working at The Memorial Sloan-Kettering Cancer Institute in New York City, while attending Union Theological Seminary, decided to spend the holidays with her mother. She also was attending the Christmas Eve Dance at the Club, but with an escort. My first look at her was spell-binding. Here was a tall (5'10 ½"), stately and gorgeous woman dressed in a black velvet sheath, wearing no makeup and no jewelry. Her black hair was parted in the center and hung naturally on each side of her beautiful face. I was awe struck! We danced a couple of dances in the early part of the evening and then, if my memory be correct, we danced most of the last part of the evening, to the exclusion of her date! For me, it was love at first sight. I asked if I might call on Christmas afternoon and was told that "tea" would be served at four. I went home alone that evening!

The home was beautiful and I was graciously received by both Chase and her mother. After "tea", as I started to depart, I was invited to have supper the next evening there at her home. It was a special evening getting to know both Chase and her mother. Upon my departure, Mary gave me a bottle of homemade scuppernong wine which had been made by Mary "for purely medicinal purposes." (In later days after our marriage, Chase told me that when her mother gave me the wine, she, Chase, knew that I was "hooked.") We had several more dates before the holidays were over and she returned to New York and I to Nashville.

During the ensuing months, we corresponded regularly until the summer of 1955 when I was re-assigned to The Engineer Center Headquarters at Fort Belvoir, Virginia. Now, being on the East Coast, I was able to drive to New York City regularly and Chase was able to take the train down to Washington, where I would meet her and take her to Alexandria, Virginia, where I had an apartment with two other First Lieutenants. I was able to arrange accommodations for Chase in our same apartment building with some Airline stewardesses my roommates and I knew. It was all quite proper.

In November of 1955, I invited Chase to meet me in Philadelphia for the Army-Navy Football Game. We also invited her New York roommate, Ginny Davidson, and my friend from Thomasville, Jack McLean, to double date with us. It was a glorious Saturday and I don't remember the score or even the victor, for what happened after the game was one of the highlights of our life together. In the Philadelphia Railroad Station, among a throng of thousands, I asked Chase to be my bride;

and when she accepted, I had in my pocket a West Point miniature ring which I placed on her finger. The remainder of that day is a blur, as she and Ginny returned by train to New York and Jack and I drove back to Washington. Jack was assigned at that time to the Office of Naval Intelligence (ONI).

The following days, weeks, and months were so complicated that I am not sure how we were able to coordinate everything that had to be done. We set a date for the wedding: 7 April 1956, in Thomasville at St. Thomas Episcopal Church. All the attendant tasks were scheduled and prioritized by Mary. Plans for pre-nuptial parties materialized. China, silver and crystal patterns were selected. The wedding party attendants were picked and asked to participate. Chase's attendants included Ginny Davidson; my sister, Nell Brannon; Harriet Hawkins and Toddy Edwards, both from Thomasville. I chose my brother-in-law, Francis Brannon, as my Best Man. Dr. Ben Grace of Thomasville was my Head Usher and the remaining Groomsmen were Jack McLean; Charles Crowder of Washington, DC, also with ONI; and one of my West Point roommates, Jack Driskill, of Louisville, Kentucky. Toddy Edward's son, David, was our acolyte for the wedding ceremony. During all these preparations and before Chase left New York City for Thomasville, Chase and I managed to see each other as often as possible. On the weekends that she would come to Washington, Mary would fly up to "chaperone", for it would not have been proper, according to Thomasville protocol, for an engaged couple to rendezvous for a weekend without a chaperone. Upon Mary's arrival in Washington, Chase and I would drive her to her accommodations where she remained the entire weekend, unbeknownst to the people of Thomasville who concerned themselves with such matters! On the weekends that I drove to New York City, I would stay nearby Chase's apartment which she shared with three other girls; and would usually have Sunday brunch at their apartment, stepping over assorted bodies left over from Saturday night. A good time was had by all and we both successfully survived the strain of waiting for the April wedding.

The day finally arrived -- 7 April 1956. The weather in Thomasville was perfect. As the appointed hour approached, the St. Thomas Episcopal Church sanctuary begin to fill and even overflowed. In fact, the windows were open and many people were standing outside looking in. Would you believe it? For more than twenty years after the ceremony, we heard from several guests still complaining that they had not been seated inside. One of the causes of such a dilemma was the fact that many of those invited to the ceremony did not respond saying that they were coming. This has always been one of my pet peeves - R.S.V.P. simply means "I would like to know if I should count on your attendance." It is a request from the inviter so that adequate food and beverage or seating will be provided. It is the only responsibility of the invitee.

The reception after the ceremony was held at The Three Toms Inn, a wonderfully quaint wooden hotel on Gordon Avenue which, unfortunately, has since burned down. In addition to the hors d'oeuvres, open-faced sandwiches, nuts and candies and of course champagne (even in Thomasville in 1956!), there was a punch bowl of delicious raspberry fruit cocktail punch for those attending who did not care for an alcoholic beverage. Of the approximately three hundred who attended, my estimate of those taking punch was - well, to be totally facetious - about two dozen!

After the wedding cake had been cut and the reception ended, both Chase and I changed into our "going away" clothes. My Super 88 Olds was brought around to the entrance. Thanks to all my groomsmen, the car was decorated with "cute" slogans, tin cans, streamers, and other assorted paraphernalia. We departed about five o'clock bound for The Cloister at Sea Island, Georgia, some one hundred seventy miles eastward on the Atlantic Coast. When we arrived in Quitman, only twenty-eight miles from Thomasville, we stopped to have the car washed and divested of all its trappings. While this was being done, Chase and I went across the street to a local café and had coffee and a bite to eat. Back on the road, we continued on to our destination.

I had purposely arranged our arrival to be at about ten o'clock so there would be little commotion in the lobby. However, the car wash had delayed our actual arrival until eleven thirty! As we entered the lobby looking as un-newly-married as possible, I proceeded to the desk to check us in, while Chase sat down in one of the easy chairs in the lobby, throwing her Spring coat over her lap. In so doing, both pockets emptied their treasures of rice all over the lobby carpet! Several bellhops came to our assistance with brooms and dustpans and even a vacuum cleaner. It was the kind of entrance we both had planned so carefully to avoid.

We finally got to our room and began to laugh uncontrollably as Chase opened her suitcase and found a plastic bag of white "sour grapes", courtesy of Ginny. Laughter turned to frustration when I was unable to find the key to my suitcase. We looked everywhere and finally found it - on my key ring! And so to bed after another round of champagne.

As the sun arose, I was hungry! I had previously arranged for our wedding breakfast to be served in our room at eight. I learned early in our courtship that neither Chase nor I were very sociable until we had had our morning coffee. At about eight-o-five, I heard the service tray coming down the hall, squeaky wheels and all. About six feet from our door, one of the wheels jammed and the attendant upset the entire cart in the hall, spilling everything, including the coffee. For the next hour until our new breakfast arrived, we managed to be both civil and sociable. In later years, we laughed on re-telling this story. But it was a very inauspicious beginning for our almost forty-five years of married life together.

The week at Sea Island was pleasant but we were unable to bathe in the surf, for the weather was miserable - cold and windy. The pool, however, was enclosed with a glass siding seaward, so we were able to enjoy it and to meet other honeymooning couples. We met one couple, the guy was about six feet and weighed about two-forty and his bride was about five feet and weighed about one hundred pounds, soaking wet. Unfortunately, she developed an impacted wisdom tooth on their wedding night and was taking some medication which immobilized her in their room, while he spent most of the day at the pool side, dangling his feet in the water and panting loudly! We three had cocktails each evening before he took dinner to their room. There were also bicycles and horses, tennis and golf, lectures and nature walks, none of which we were able to fit into our schedule. It was a most wonderful honeymoon.

📖📖📖

When we returned to Virginia, our first home was the apartment I had previously shared with the two other Lieutenants, both of whom were married about the same time as I. It was a remarkable discovery that the three of us bachelors could occupy a one room efficiency with a small bath and one closet, but Chase and I had no room for anything.

We three guys had slept on Hollywood beds and used our footlockers as chairs and tables; but when Chase arrived with her crinoline skirts, gowns and dresses, hat boxes, shoes, bags, et cetera, there didn't seem to be any room for my uniforms or me. This lasted only a few weeks until I was able to secure quarters on post at Fort Belvoir where I was serving as Aide-de-Camp to the Deputy Commanding General, among my other assigned duties.

Our new quarters consisted of a quadruplex two-storied barracks, with a furnace for the steam heat located next to our first floor bedroom. At times, even in the dead of winter, when the furnace had been banked on Friday evening for the weekend, Chase and I had to sleep with the bedroom windows open, in order to survive. These barracks had been built in 1919 as a hospital, condemned in 1939, renovated and occupied by us in 1956. There was a urinal behind the door in the kitchen in which Chase planted ivy! The living room-dining room combination had a post in the center which defied rugs of any large dimension; and the room contained five windows, all of a different size. I was able to get a supply of (unused!) target cloth from the Firing Range Officer so that Chase could make curtains. I forgot to tell her to wash the material first to get out the sizing. The first batch of curtains shrank approximately thirty percent. The next set looked great.

Being an Aide at Belvoir had its moments. I enjoyed meeting all the dignitaries of the world who came to Washington and were shuttled out to Belvoir for a parade and dinner, but Chase had to become involved in all the women's activities by virtue of my position. On one occasion, she was chosen to model for a furrier who came on post to sell his wares to the Officer's wives. She looked magnificent in a white fox fur. But the incident that we remembered and re-told again and again was the reception at the Officer's Club for the Spring Tea. The wife of the ranking Colonel on post poured coffee by virtue of his position, and the wife of the youngest Second Lieutenant poured tea. During a lull in the pourings, "Mrs. Colonel" turned to her young associate and proudly inquired,

"My husband is a full Colonel, and yours?"

To which the young lady responded,

"My husband is twenty-two, and yours?"

⁂

In August of 1956, four months after our wedding, Chase and I were invited by a Thomasville friend, whose two sons had been married that same Spring, to vacation at their retreat in Canada, just the six of us "honeymooners." The mother of the two boys had purchased an island from the Canadian government in upper Ontario and had built a main cabin containing a big room with a fireplace and room to eat, a kitchen, and one bedroom and one bath. In addition, she had built two cabins, each of which consisted of a bedroom and a bath. The heating unit in the cabins was a wood stove. Chase and I drove from Fort Belvoir in Virginia to New York City, then along the entire length of the New York State Thruway to Buffalo where we crossed into Canada. Around Lake Ontario, through Hamilton, we arrived at Toronto, where we "turned left" and headed northward up Route 11, all the way to North Bay. Just south of North Bay we stopped to see the home of the Dionne Family, whose quintuplets had been born just one week after I: on 28 May 1930.

Continuing up Highway 11 for another seventy-five miles or so, we arrived at the village of Temagami where we parked our car and were met by the two boys, our hosts. Boarding their motor boat with our luggage, we traveled to their island in Lake Temagami. The island was approximately two acres and was covered with blueberries. On the afternoon of our arrival, the six of us sat on the dock, having cocktails, and listening to the loons. We three guys agreed that, while the girls slept-in the next morning, we would go "skinny-dipping" at dawn. My swim lasted but a few seconds for my "friends" failed to mention that there had been ice on the lake up until the 4th of July! We managed to warm up enough to pick a few pints of blueberries so that the girls could make blueberry pancakes for breakfast. When we needed supplies, or just wanted to go souvenir-shopping, we would paddle a canoe over to Bear Island, another island within the Lake, where there was an Indian Trading Post.

The main cabin had a gasoline-powered refrigerator and a gas stove. There was also a zither in the cabin, so I managed to compose a few songs in my quiet moments. We were so far north that we were not able to receive anything on our radios. When our ten-day vacation ended and we had returned to the village of Temagami and "civilization", we learned that three significant world events had occurred: (1) Adlai Stevenson had said that he would not be a candidate for the Presidency of the United States; (2) Gamal Abdel Nasser, the President of Egypt, had scuttled the Suez Canal; and (3) the Italian liner, Andrea Doria, had sunk. It was amazing to find that the life of the world continues without my input!

Life at Fort Belvoir continued apace until January of 1957, when it became obvious to me that I would be a First Lieutenant for quite a while. Since the Korean War had ended in 1953, most all promotions had ceased. The Army just had too many Officers. (My West Point Classmates did not get promoted to the rank of Captain until seven years after our graduation.) I decided that I had had all the Army experience possible up to that time; and at age twenty-seven, I was eager to do more than the Army would apparently allow. I requested an appointment with the Chief of Engineers, Major General Emerson C. Itschner, West Point Class of 1924, so that I might submit my resignation from the Army. Upon being received in his office, he proceeded to tell me why he would not approve my request for resignation. He repeated the litany of my assignments and my experiences: Platoon and Company Commander in Combat; Aides-de-Camp to the Commanding Generals of the 45th and 24th Divisions in Korea and the Deputy Commanding General at Fort Belvoir; Assistant G-3 of the Belvoir Post for Bands and Protocol; Assistant to the Secretary of the Post General Staff; a graduate of the Advanced Engineering Course; and selection to be a White House Aide in the Administration of President Eisenhower, which I had declined because Chase and I were being married and, at that time, married Aides in the White House were not acceptable. In addition, said General Itschner, "With your OEI (Officer Efficiency Index), I cannot justify your release." After much discussion about my future, the General suggested that I talk with the Chief. (General Maxwell D. Taylor was now the Chief of Staff of the U.S. Army, having previously served as Commander of the 8th U.S. Army in Korea and before that as the Superintendent at West Point when I was a Cadet.) Having mentioned President Eisenhower, I want to add that his son, John, had been my English Instructor at West Point; and while his father was in the White House, John and his family were living at Fort Belvoir, as he had been designated the Infantry

Liaison to The White House. Chase and I saw John and Barbara quite often at the Officers Club; and I, along with two Secret Service agents, had taught young David to swim, in the Officers Club pool.

During his Administration, President Eisenhower visited Thomasville on several occasions, to hunt quail and to play golf. His Secretary of the Treasury, George M. Humphrey, owned a plantation south of Thomasville called "Milestone." "Ike", as he was affectionately known to almost everyone, spoke highly of the Glen Arven course and liked to say that it was in Thomasville that he "honed his game."

Other Presidents have also visited Thomasville. When William McKinley was nominated to be the President of the United States on the Republican ticket, he was visiting in the City at the home of Mark Hanna, a winter resident from Ohio, who was known as "the maker of Presidents." During his Administration, President McKinley visited Thomasville several times. As did President and Mrs. Carter.

📖 📖 📖

General Maxwell D. Taylor was one of the most brilliant men I have ever known. In addition, he was a linguist, being fluent in eight languages. At our meeting in the Pentagon, after I had explained to him my dilemma, he suggested that since I was conversant in both French and Russian, my talents might be used in areas other than the Combat Arms. My training at West Point had been chiefly in Electrical Engineering with side emphasis on Chemistry and Mathematics. (I had been invited to return to West Point as an Instructor in Mathematics, but that assignment had not been approved by the Corps of Engineers since, in their opinion, such a tour of duty would not enhance my progress in the Corps.) After some discussion and planning for future service to my country, I resigned my Regular Army Commission and received a Reserve Commission with no loss in relative rank position. These changes in Army status were contingent on my receiving an offer of employment with the International Business Machines Corporation to work on the Classified SAGE project which was the U.S. Air Force Project that tied together all the radar sites in North America (the Dew Line) and the twenty-four computerized SAGE sites across the northern part of the United States, which controlled all aircraft and missiles under one umbrella and one command. (SAGE was the acronym for Semi-Automatic Ground Environment.) I was tentatively offered a position with IBM and proceeded to Kingston, New York, for my interview, which resulted in an offer of employment, to begin immediately. (I think somebody had talked to somebody else.) Chase and I departed Belvoir and moved to Lake Katrine, a suburb of Kingston. We purchased our first home. It was a three bedroom, one bath, living room, kitchen with dishwasher and freezer, and dining area, family room, laundry room with washer and dryer, an attached one-car garage, the whole house being air conditioned, on a lot size 200' x 220'. The price: $18,500. Remember this was 1957! Our first son, Richard Renz, was born in the Kingston Hospital on the snowy, full moon night of 15 March 1958. Chase's mother, Mary, had come up from Thomasville to be with us at that time. Several days before Rich's arrival, the three of us went out to dinner at the Rathskeller in Kingston. On that particular night, the special was "Southern Fried Chicken." Mary decided to order the special. When her plate was served and she had cut into the chicken, she discovered that it had been heavily breaded and fried to a crisp but that the chicken inside was only partially cooked. Upon summoning the waiter, Mary replied, "Please return this to the chef and tell him that this chicken doesn't have even a speaking acquaintance with the South." So much for Northern cooking.

While we were in Kingston, some one hundred miles north of New York City, we were able to drive to the City to attend dinners with friends and the theatre. During our residency in Kingston, the West Point Society of New York City gave a dinner at The Waldorf-Astoria Hotel, featuring as guests all five-star Army Generals and all West Point recipients of the Congressional Medal of Honor. Seated on the dais that evening was General of the Army Omar N. Bradley and his West Point Classmate, the President of the United States, Dwight D. Eisenhower. The other notables were the recipients of the Medal of Honor. The Master of Ceremonies was Bob Hope, who, in making his introductions of the Head Table, never mentioned any of the highlights of their careers, but instead, talked about their golf games, having played with everyone on the dais. Each introduction was hilarious. When Bob finished his introductions, he had overlooked introducing Ike before he sat down. A titter of uneasiness ran through the audience. Finally, Bob leaned over to the microphone, not getting out of his chair, and said, "Oh, you all know Ike." The laughter was loud and prolonged, led by the President.

The SAGE computer was a fascinating machine. At each of the twenty-four sites across the nation, there were two computers, officially known as ANFSQ-7, each of which had about forty-three thousand, five hundred vacuum tubes. One could prove mathematically that the machine would not operate because one is too busy changing tubes. However, because of the triple-redundancy built into each machine, we were able to achieve better than 99.6% efficiency. When a plane was "scrambled" in an alert for an incoming, over-the-pole missile, the plane would "lock on" the missile and the computer would guide the plane in its pursuit.

If the plane crossed the border between two sectors, the adjoining computer would pick up that plane and continue to monitor and guide it. After a successful mission, the computer would look at the fuel level in the plane and guide it to the nearest landing field for refueling. It was a most complex and wonderfully designed system. After my initial training in Kingston, I was re-assigned to Madison, Wisconsin, to the SAGE site at Truax Airfield. Chase and I, with young Rich, sold our home in Lake Katrine, for $22,500 after only eleven months and took the washer, the dryer and the freezer with us! I decided that there was money to be made in real estate!

We purchased a house under construction on Pheasant Hill Road in Madison, and, upon its completion, we moved in. In Kingston, we had made lots of friends and were close by to friends and loved ones on the East Coast. But in Madison, we knew no one except the mother of Chase's classmate at Smith, where they had gone to college. At Christmastime, Mary came up again from Thomasville and we were all invited to Christmas dinner at the home of Chase's classmate. On the way over, Mary said, "I do hope they don't have goose and sauerkraut, for that was the traditional dinner at Mother Berger's for years." After sherry in the living room, as we proceeded to the dining room, the hostess said, "I hope you like goose and sauerkraut. It is traditional in our family." We all enjoyed it immensely, particularly I, who has hated sauerkraut since birth.

While in Madison, my visits to the SAGE sites took me as far west as Minot, North Dakota, and southward to Kansas City, Chase's birthplace. On one trip to Grand Forks, North Dakota, I started out by airplane from Madison to Duluth, Minnesota, where the plane was grounded because of snow. I had an appointment the next morning at nine in Grand Forks with General Thomas White, Commander of the Strategic Air Command. It was a very important meeting and I knew that General White expected me to be there. So I rented a car and drove through the snow from Duluth to Grand Forks, a distance of approximately two hundred, seventy-five miles, arriving at about eight in the morning. When I arrived at the meeting, the General asked about my trip. I explained my course of action as the other attendees were gathering, all except the Base Commander, who sent word that he was snowbound in his driveway! General White was not amused and said so both verbally and in writing. In later years, General White became the Chief of Staff of the United States Air Force.

One December morning in Madison, I awoke at the usual time to find that our bedroom was totally dark. I went into the kitchen to make the coffee and noted sunlight streaming into the room. I then put on my snow boots and went outside to find eight feet of drifted snow covering our bedroom window. It was at breakfast that morning that the decision was made to leave Madison. This Southerner had taken about all he could and longed for the heat and humidity of the South. Inquiries were made and it was determined that a position existed for me in Washington, DC., not truly the South but a step in the right direction. My new assignment would be as Administrative Assistant to the President of the Federal Systems Division (FSD) of IBM. FSD was responsible for the manufacturing, programming and servicing of all the computers IBM sold to the Department of Defense. My new office was located in Rockville, Maryland, so Chase and I decided to rent for a year, to get the lay of the land and community and school structure. We rented a three bedroom house in Chevy Chase, Maryland, just over the District line. It was a three story, white brick home owned by a widowed Russian who served us tea from her samovar in her dacha, centered on the block where our home and three others were located. I also got to practice the Russian language. It was during this time that our second son was born, on the weekend of the Cherry Blossom Festival in Washington. When Chase's labor started, the ambulance arrived with three young men in their early twenties who informed us that traffic was quite heavy in the District. We were headed for Doctors' Hospital, which was located only three blocks from the White House. As the ambulance progressed down Connecticut Avenue and Chase's pains became closer together, the pace of the ambulance was slowed by the crowds in the streets. She became quite upset, voicing her concern that she just might have this baby in the middle of Connecticut Avenue attended by three kids who had just started shaving. However, we all arrived at the Hospital in time for the arrival, on 5 April 1959, of David Shepherd. My mother, Clara, had come from Thomasville to be with us for this event. All went well and we all returned to Chevy Chase after a few days.

With our family growing, we decided to move farther out of the metropolitan area, so we bought a house in Bethesda on Seneca Lane near the National Institutes of Health. This was a lovely little home with a large back yard in a quiet neighborhood. So we thought! One Saturday evening, our next door neighbor's house was trashed, with the sofa cushions and the beds being torn up in an obvious search for drugs. Chase also was pregnant again, so it appeared to be a good time to move to a larger house.

We looked at many homes in Montgomery County, Maryland, and several subdivisions of established homes. None quite suited us. Finally, we found a new subdivision called Old Farm located in North Bethesda (although it used a Rockville Post Office address), about thirteen miles northwest of the zero mile marker behind the White House in

Washington, DC. One of the homes under construction was almost exactly what Chase and I were looking for, so we made a few changes here and there: expanded the patio to double size, moved the fireplace from the living room to the family room, added a garage and agreed on a price. We had just sold our home in Bethesda for $25,900 and the price we agreed on for the new home was $37,950. (We later added an arbor over the patio with the help of a neighbor.) Chase was very distraught that we could not afford such extravagance. But with a helpful builder, we put down five shares of IBM stock and took out a thirty year loan for $32,000 at 5%. "We will never pay this off", she cried, and I do mean cried. "We are getting in over our head, with a third child coming soon." Jumping ahead, I am pleased to say that we refinanced twice, sent all three boys to colleges and graduate schools and paid off the house loan in 1983.

William Postell was born on 26 December 1961. Mary was again visiting us and we had just finished Christmas dinner and had gotten the two boys to bed, the dishes washed and had settled in the family room when Chase said "I'm ready. Let's go." We arrived at the hospital in Bethesda about ten thirty Christmas night and Bill was born at two thirty the next morning. All went well until we had arrived back in Old Farm and Mary had gone home and the snow began to fall. It snowed and it snowed for two days. Old Farm at that time was a developing community with a plan for about five hundred homes. When we moved in, in September, 1961, we were the seventh house to be completed. By December, there were other homes in various stages of construction and occupation, but no paved roads. After the snow subsided, the road in front of our house had approximately four feet of drifted snow, making any idea of a plow or any motor vehicle impractical. To add to this condition, all electricity in the area was out due to ice on the power lines. Fortunately, our new neighbors across the street had a gas stove. So the men of both houses began to dig a passageway between our respective front doors. When completed it provided an avenue of access for heating Bill's bottles. I would take a bottle across the street and when it was hot enough, my neighbor would trudge back across with "din-din for the wee one." Since we had no electricity, we closed the doors to the library and kitchen, built a fire in the fireplace in the family room, which we had previously and fortunately moved from the living room, and cooked our meager meals over a roaring fire. It also was great for toasting marshmallows. At night, Bill was wrapped in his bassinet, Rich and Dave in sleeping bags in front of the fire, Chase on the sofa, and Dad in his easy chair. We rang in the New Year in great style. After a few more days, the snow plow arrived, the electricity was restored and our "camping out" came to an end. We lived here, at 12011 Old Bridge Road, for forty years until after Chase's death and my subsequent move back to Thomasville.

After my parents were divorced in 1950, both my parents re-married, although my mother's new marriage lasted only a few weeks. My father's new wife was Pearl Golden, a widow from Pavo whom he had known for many years. Pearl had six children, five of them were foster, and now all of them were grown with families of their own. On 3 July 1962, my father was diagnosed with lung cancer. He spent a few weeks in the Veterans Hospital in Augusta, Georgia, and then I brought him by ambulance to Archbold Memorial Hospital in Thomasville, where he remained until his death on 3 October 1962. His remains were buried in the Salem Baptist Church cemetery, where also reside the remains of his mother and her parents. My father had had a long life of varied experiences. He enrolled in Norman Park (Georgia) Junior College in 1914 at the age of twenty-five. He was recruited for the football team. During the first game in which he played, he broke his jaw, which required surgery, and which ended his football career. In the early summer of 1918, he enlisted in the United States Army and was sent to Camp Wheeler outside Macon, Georgia. He and my mother had been married on 28 April 1918, just before he was inducted into the Army. He had received his orders for France just a few weeks before the Armistice was signed, so he never had any overseas service. However, he was active in the American Legion in Thomasville and treasured his association with the other veterans in the city. Mother too was active in the Legion Auxiliary.

One December, I forget which one, I invited my father to come to Washington and travel with me to Philadelphia for the Army-Navy Football Game. He traveled from Thomasville to Washington on the train. On the Friday before the game, I purposefully drove us both into downtown Washington at rush hour so he could experience what I had to put up with daily. When we returned home that evening, I asked him what he thought of Washington traffic. His response was enlightening. "Reminds me of Court week in Thomasville." Now that's heavy traffic!!

📖 📖 📖

During the next three years, my work with IBM continued. I was chosen to attend the IBM Management School at Sands Point, New York. I also was given the opportunity to attend the Rutgers University course in International Banking and Finance, which was conducted on the campus of Princeton University. After leaving the position of Administrative Assistant to the President of the FSD after eighteen months, I was assigned to the IBM office in downtown Washington, DC, with the responsibility of monitoring IBM's contract with the U.S. Army, to build, program and service mobile computers. During the 1962 Cuban Missile Crisis, IBM received a letter from the Department of Defense, directing that an IBM 1401 Disc System be mounted in three mobile Army vans, which were provided by the Army and moved to the Homestead Air Force Base near Miami, Florida, with "the possibility of overseas deployment." I received my orders to supervise the movement and the deployment of the equipment. Part of our assigned tasks was to place, on the computer, dossiers of all Cuban-Americans residing in the United States, whom we readily identified. We, of course, did not go into Cuba; and after the crisis had ended, we returned the three vans to Fortress Monroe, Virginia, where the Army continued to test the feasibility of mobile computers for combat.

In July of 1964, General Harkins retired from the U.S. Army. His last assignment was Commander, United States Military Assistance Command, Vietnam, our first Commander in the Vietnam War. On the occasion of his retirement, an Award Ceremony and Dinner were given by President Johnson in the White House. Chase and I received an invitation, with an addendum addressed to Master Richard Renz Raiford, the Godson of General Harkins. The day of these events followed by one day the nomination by the President of General Maxwell D. Taylor, Retired, to be the United States Ambassador to Vietnam. After the award to General Harkins of another Distinguished Service Medal (his third) in the East Room, the guests proceeded to the Dining Room.

Since Rich, age six years, was the only child present, he was escorted to the Dining Room by President Johnson on his right and General (now Ambassador) Taylor on his left. When asked by the President what he thought we might have to eat, Rich promptly said "peanut butter and jelly." When we were seated, in front of him was a small plate of peanut butter and jelly sandwiches! I thought: Oh, what an attentive , alert Aide-de-Camp.

When Rich was about three or perhaps four, Chase would leave Dave and Bill with a sitter and she and Rich would travel to Georgetown in the District of Columbia for lunch with a friend from Thomasville whose husband was stationed in the Pentagon. She, her husband and I had attended Thomasville High School together, and it was a pleasure to see them again in the Washington area. She and Chase, Rich and her daughter, would go to a park in Georgetown that had slides and sand boxes, there to have their lunch. It was in that park that they met the wife of a young Senator from Massachusetts and their daughter. The three wives and their children became friends and saw each other often in the park. It was not until years later that I had the pleasure of working for her husband when he became the President of the United States, John Fitzgerald Kennedy.

After the assassination of the President, Jacqueline Bouvier Kennedy came to Thomasville as a guest, for several weeks, at Greenwood Plantation, the home of Ambassador John Hay Whitney, who had been the United States Ambassador to the Court of St. James (Great Britain) in the

Administration of her husband. While she attended Mass each morning at Saint Augustine Catholic Church, the townspeople of Thomasville were most respectful of her privacy.

📖📖📖

At this juncture of my career, a significant change occurred. I left the employment of IBM and, by invitation, became a stock broker in Washington, DC, with the firm of Ferris & Company, where I remained for about six years. During these years, I attended the Wharton School of Finance for three summers; Georgetown University in Washington, DC, to study Pure Mathematics; and The George Washington University in the District of Columbia to study Russian Language and Literature, the latter two schools at night. In addition, I studied with and was registered by the New York Institute of Finance, a requirement for my New York Stock Exchange license.

In 1965, I had the honor of serving on the Security Detail for the Inaugural Balls of President Johnson. I had gotten to know the President through a rather circuitous route. The President's daughter, Linda Bird, was dating Marine Captain Chuck Robb (who later became a United States Senator from the State of Virginia) whom I had met through a Navy friend who was a graduate of Annapolis and who became a client of mine at Ferris and Company. Linda and Chuck had dined at our home in Rockville on several occasions, and we had also become bridge partners. Linda too became a client of mine at Ferris. When the President asked me to serve during his Inaugural Balls, I naturally accepted but inquired how he had "found" me. The President replied that he knew I was a graduate of West Point, that I spoke Russian, and that Linda said I was a "helluva" stock broker. When Linda married Chuck, Chase and I were invited to their wedding in The White House. It was a splendid affair. After the ceremony in the East Room, the chairs were removed and the dancing began. Peter Duchin (Eddie's son) and his Orchestra were the featured musicians. Of the many guests present, the one who stood out was Carol Channing, mainly because of her attire. She wore yellow bloomers adorned with yellow ostrich plumes. I excused myself from the company of my wife and went over to the Orchestra. I asked Peter if he would play a "Charleston" so I could dance with Miss Channing. She graciously accepted my invitation; and as we began to dance, the remainder of the guests cleared the dance floor. It was an exciting experience, one that I shall always remember fondly. When I had thanked my dance partner and returned to my wife, I found her cowering in the corner of the room, trying not to be associated with the "showoff."

On a later occasion, Chase and I were invited to the White House for bridge in the family quarters. One of the other couples present was Ambassador Osman and his wife, The Princess Lalla Nezha, the daughter of the King of Morocco. When the rotation paired the Raifords with the Royal couple, there was a brief pause of silence after the bidding, awaiting the lead from the Princess. When I said, "Its your lead, Princess", my dear wife said, "Oh how sweet of you." No one laughed.

On 15 May 1966, Sylvanus Thayer, the Father of the Military Academy, was inducted into the Hall of Fame for Great Americans at New York

University in New York City. The Committee formed to promote his selection for induction was chaired by Lieutenant General Willis Crittenberger, a graduate in West Point's Class of 1913. There were several senior military members on the Committee and a few non-graduates of West Point, to include Mr. John Lodge. General Crittenberger asked me to be his Assistant, his "Aide-de-Camp" so to speak. I was honored to do so and readily accepted his invitation. As it so happened, a descendant of Sylvanus Thayer, John Thayer, was my next-door neighbor in Old Farm, so we traveled to New York together for the ceremony.

On 27 January 1967, the Space Capsule containing the three Astronauts, Edward H. White, II, Gus Grissom, and Roger Chaffee, caught fire on the pad at Cape Canaveral, Florida, and burned, killing all three Astronauts. Ed White was a classmate of mine at West Point, and we had run track together. It was Ed who helped me to perfect my form in the high hurdles. In a previous space flight, in June of 1965, he had become the first American to walk in space. Less than one week before this tragedy, Ed had telephoned me at my home to discuss some investments on which I was advising him. When I hung up the phone and returned to the dinner table, all three boys, as if rehearsed, shouted "Ed White, the As-tro-naut." A few days after the tragedy, Ed's funeral was conducted at West Point and burial was in the Old Cemetery. Prior to the burial, there was a reception in Cullum Hall which was attended by Classmates, wives, military personnel, Space Center personnel and a host of friends. Representing the Administration was The Vice President of the United States, Hubert H. Humphrey. We spoke briefly that day, having previously met on several occasions. About four months later, Chase and I were at The White House for dinner and, during the cocktail hour before the dinner, we were chatting with Mrs. Humphrey when Senator Everett M. Dirksen joined us and asked if we had seen his wife. I replied to the Senator that Mrs. Dirksen was near the window of the room talking with Ambassador Perle Mesta. "I should have been able to locate her," he said "'cause she is with the ugliest woman here." Ambassador Mesta was not known for her beauty, but for her intellect and tact. After The Senator had left to find his wife, The Vice President walked up. Mrs. Humphrey said, "Hubert, I would like for you to know the Raifords." Shaking hands, he said, "Oh, I know Bill and Chase well. He is a classmate of Ed White." What a memory! I truly believe that he and Governor Stevenson of Illinois were the last two "statesmen" produced by this Republic.

During a dinner in Washington, DC, when the Vice President was the speaker of the evening, his talk was rather long, as was usually the case. When he finally finished speaking and returned to his seat on the dais, Mrs. Humphrey, not knowing that the microphone in front of her was "live", said "Hubert, you don't have to be eternal to be immortal." Everyone, including the Vice President, laughed heartily.

On another occasion, at a dinner in Washington when Illinois Governor Adlai E. Stevenson was the Democratic candidate for President of the United States, Chase and I were in attendance because she had been a classmate of Nancy's at Smith. Nancy was the wife of the younger Adlai, the son of the Governor. During the "Question and Answer" period which followed the dinner, the Governor was asked for his definition of a diplomat. He responded that when a diplomat says "yes", he really means "maybe." When he says "maybe", he really means "no." But when he says "no", he ceases to be a diplomat.

CLASS I, UNP. No. 2948

COPYRIGHT OFFICE
OF THE UNITED STATES OF AMERICA

THE LIBRARY OF CONGRESS :: WASHINGTON

CERTIFICATE OF COPYRIGHT REGISTRATION

This is to certify, in conformity with section 55 of the Act to Amend and Consolidate the Acts respecting Copyright, approved March 4, 1909, as amended by the Act approved March 2, 1913, that a photograph or other identifying reproduction of the

drawing

OF A SCIENTIFIC OR TECHNICAL CHARACTER, named herein, not reproduced for sale, has been deposited in this Office under the provisions of the Act of 1909, and that registration of a claim to copyright for the first term of twenty-eight years has been duly made in the name of

William Russell Raiford,
407 North Crawford St., Thomasville, Ga.

Title: The Trisection of an angle.
By William Russell Raiford, of United States.

Copy received   June 1, 1947

[SEAL]

Sam B. Warner
Register of Copyrights

THE COPYRIGHT

Reprinted from the AMERICAN MATHEMATICAL MONTHLY
Vol. 68, No. 9, November, 1961

AN APPROXIMATE TRISECTION

WILLIAM R. RAIFORD, IBM, Washington, D.C.

The simple ruler-and-compass constructions indicated in the figure give an approximate trisection of an angle $0° \leq \theta \leq 240°$. We have

$$\frac{AC}{AB} = \tan \psi = \cot \tfrac{3}{4}\theta (\cos \theta - 1) + \sin \theta.$$

The error, $\psi - \tfrac{1}{3}\theta$, computed on the IBM 709 for each degree, indicates that it is monotonic increasing, is $0°21'40''$ at $\theta = 90°$, is $3°26'6''$ at $\theta = 180°$, and is $10°0'0''$ at $\theta = 240°$.

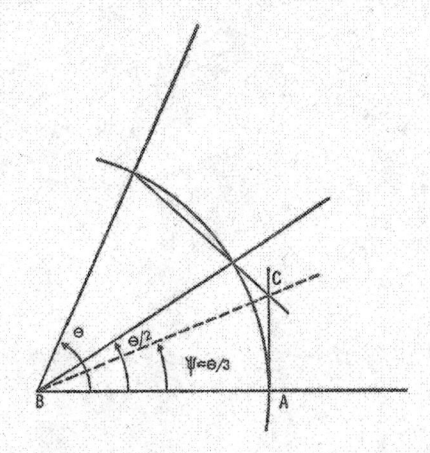

THE TRISECTION

CARNEGIE HALL TICKETS TO NEW YORK GOVERNOR THOMAS E. DEWEY

Korea 1953

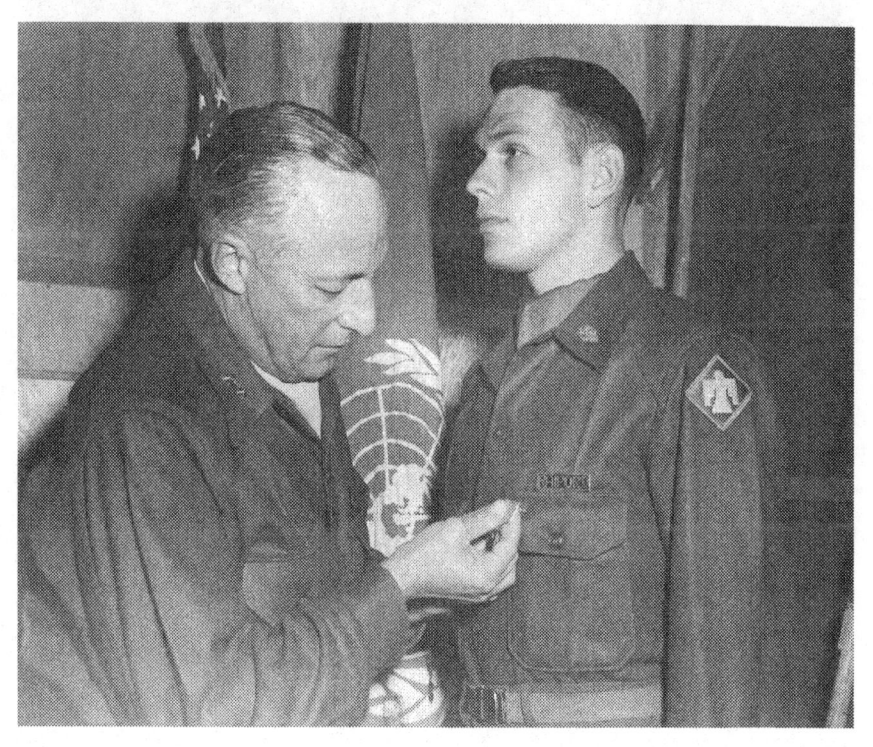

Award of the Bronze Star

GENERAL MAXWELL D. TAYLOR

CUMBERLAND LOCKS AT NASHVILLE, TENNESSEE

CHASE AND BILL

Dressed for a Formal Presentation

Gen. Omar Bradley, The Author, Mr. John Lodge and
Gen. Willis Crittenberger

THE AUTHOR WITH WARREN BEATTY

*To William Raiford
With best wishes,* Ronald Reagan

PRESIDENT RONALD REAGAN AND THE AUTHOR

THE DIAMOND EAGLE OF THE SOCIETY OF THE CINCINNATI

H R H Louis de Bourbon at Versailles on The Day of My Award of The Legion of Honor

318 Warren Avenue

The Author at Christmastime 2006

On one of our family vacation trips, this one in 1969, we drove our station wagon from our home in Maryland to Montreal and Quebec City, where we visited with a French banker whom I knew. His family had already gone from the city to their summer home down the St. Lawrence River near San Simeon. After a two hundred mile drive down the river and a brief visit with the family, we boarded the auto-ferry for the trip across the River to Rivière-du-Loup. We then traveled down Canadian Highway 2 to Fredericton, New Brunswick, and then south to Saint John. After checking into our motel, we made arrangements for a fishing trip the next morning to nearby Lake Benton. While the three boys and I rowed out into the lake, Chase remained on the shore, to read and nap. When we returned to the shore, Chase said that she was unable to nap because of the noise caused by the sinker which "ker-plopped" with each baiting. That was the best example of "silence and remoteness" I could ever recall.

From Saint John, we drove first to the edge of the Bay of Fundy to watch the forty-foot tides; then on to Moncton to see the tidal bore; and then around the Bay of Fundy to a wonderfully rustic lodge at Parrsboro on Minas Basin. This was the summer home of one of Canada's former Prime Ministers. The boys enjoyed gathering rough amethysts which had washed up on the shore in front of the lodge. From there we drove through Truro down to Halifax, Nova Scotia, stopping at our motel in Dartmouth, a nearby town. This was a particularly eventful evening, for it was the night that the first American walked on the moon. We all sat in rapt attention in our motel room and observed everything on our black and white television set. The next day, we took a side trip down to the lovely coastal village of Peggy's Cove. It was here that I purchased an oil of the coastline from a native artist, and the five of us took a tour of a salmon processing plant. On one of the evenings in Dartmouth, we were invited to the home of a Canadian friend who was posted to the Embassy in Washington, DC, and who lived down the street from our home in Old Farm. The menu consisted of shrimp and lobster, crab claws and scallops, baked beans and slaw, and baked potatoes and cold beer. The home was perched on a bluff overlooking the Atlantic Ocean. Not only was the meal terrific, but the view from the front yard was breath-taking. We really hated to leave!

The next day we drove along the northern coast of Nova Scotia to the port of Digby which is the home of the Atlantic Scallop Fleet. We stood on the pier awaiting the ships, and when they arrived, we purchased a bushel of scallops and took them to one of the restaurants nearby and proceeded to consume our entire haul! While in that area, we also visited the Port Royal National Historic Site. This is a truly magnificent re-constructed fort with all the original details having been perfectly restored. Continuing on around the coast to Yarmouth, we drove our station wagon onto The Blue Nose, a ferry that took us across the Gulf of Maine on an overnight trip to Bar Harbor. When we debarked, we headed down the coast of Maine on U.S. Highway 1, stopping at the most picturesque town of Camden. The trip from Bar Harbor to Boston took longer than we had anticipated, because of Chase's love of lobsters. I have lost count of the stops we made, but they all tasted so good. We finally got home to Maryland and all agreed that this was one of our best family vacations.

Another of the many trips that Chase and I took with our three boys was to California in 1971. We flew from Dulles International Airport outside Washington, DC, to San Francisco. After getting settled in our motel room, we picked up our rental car and drove into the "City By The Bay", exploring the usual tourist sites: riding the cable cars, having a snack at Fisherman's Wharf, climbing Nob Hill. The next day we drove across The Golden Gate Bridge to Marin County, visiting Sausalito and Muir Woods, climbing Mount Tamalpais, and then driving across the Richmond-San Rafael Bridge to the city of Richmond to visit with the family of one of my West Point roommates who had been killed in an airplane accident at Christmastime, 1951. We all had dinner in Berkeley and watched the "hippies" on the campus, after which we drove across the Bay Bridge back to our motel at the airport. The following day we got tickets to a baseball game in Candlestick Park. We had been warned about the sudden changes in temperature, so we purchased long underwear in the City and took a thermos of hot chocolate with us. This was the 27th of July! It reminded me of Mark Twain's comment that the coldest winter he had ever spent was a summer in San Francisco. When the fog rolled in, you literally could not see the players on the field.

On our last day in San Francisco, we picked up our rental Winnebago and began our trip down the coast, visiting friends in Aptos (the wife being the sister of another West Point classmate who had been killed in the same airplane crash in 1951) and spending the first night parked in the yard of friends in Portola Valley. The father was the son of one of my clients in Washington, DC, who had married one of Chase's childhood friends from Kansas City, Missouri. Their two sons took our three boys in tow, enjoying the pool, the dogs and bows and arrows. The next day we drove down Highway 1 to the Monterey Peninsular, stopping for lunch with Society of the Cincinnati friends at Pebble Beach. Their home was on the 16th hole of the Pebble Beach Golf Course where they often set up a cocktail bar and invited players in for a drink during their play. After our host took us for a ride on the Seventeen Mile Drive and then lunch at "the Club", we continued southward, stopping overnight at Big Sur. It was fun climbing up the sides of the river to the Falls and then seeing all the "hippies" of all ages sunning themselves "au naturel" on the rocks.

The next morning we continued down the coast to the Hearst Castle at San Simeon, then onward to Santa Barbara, where we visited the home of a friend, a U.S. Olympic Gold Medal Decathlete. We finally ended our coastal drive at an RV Park near Disneyland. It took us two days to cover "everything" but we managed to do so. On our final day in California, we drove the Winnebago to its "turn in" point and took a mini-bus to the Los Angeles Airport, where we boarded a 747 for our flight back to Dulles. The flight was the second scheduled transcontinental flight for this aircraft, and we made the trip, coast-to-coast, from take-off to touch-down, in three hours and fifty-nine minutes! The boys and I enjoyed going to the upper lounge and listening to the piano player on the baby grand, but Chase would not leave her seat, saying that she was afraid that the plane would be top heavy and might tip over!

📖📖📖

In 1970, I left the brokerage business and was invited to join the Investment Management firm of Loomis Sayles and Company in Washington, DC. At that time I was assigned portfolio management over about twenty accounts totaling approximately one hundred million dollars. I was awarded the designation of Chartered Investment Counselor by The Investment Counsel Association of America in 1972; and was elected a Fellow of the Financial Analysts Federation in 1974. I remained with this firm for eleven years, being elected a Senior Partner in 1979.

In 1972, I was elected by my West Point Classmates for a ten-year term as President of our Class. What a great honor to be selected by your peers for such a position. I have always been extremely proud to be a member of the Class of 1952, one of the truly great classes to come out of the Academy. As just one example of the achievements of my classmates, over the years of their collective services, one has been awarded the Medal of Honor, one the Presidential Medal of Freedom, one the Air Force Cross, one the Army Distinguished Service Cross, and thirty-nine classmates have been awarded the Silver Star Medal for bravery in combat. Of those thirty-nine, five have received the award twice, five have received it three times, one has received it four times, and one, a total of five times.

In 1977, I was elected a Trustee of the U.S. Military Academy's Association of Graduates, and I remained a Trustee until 1992, when I was designated a Trustee Emeritus. During my service on the Board of Trustees, I served on the Executive and Finance Committees, from 1978 until 1992. I also was elected a Member of The West Point Alumni Foundation in 1978 and continued on that Board until 1989.

I was elected to the Board of Governors of the West Point Society of the District of Columbia, from 1962 until 1967, and again from 1973 until 1977. During my tenures on the Board, I served as Treasurer, Secretary and Vice-President of the Society, and in 1976, was elected its President. I was invited to become a member of the Washington Institute of Foreign Affairs in 1978 and remained a member until 1997. This is an organization comprised of former Ambassadors, Attachés, Senior Military Officers, Pulitzer Prize Winners, University Presidents and a few like me who just tag along for the ride.

During my tenure as President of the West Point Society of Washington, DC, I approached one of our more senior members, Major General Ulysses S. Grant, III, retired, the grandson of President Grant, and himself a graduate of the Academy in the Class of 1903. I asked the General if he would autograph my copy of the two volumes of his grandfather's Personal Memoirs. (The reason for my interest in President Grant was the fact that his wife, Julia Dent, was the college roommate of the great-great-grandmother of my wife, Chase.) The General agreed and wrote in volume one the following: "...in appreciation of his thoughtful contribution to my Grandmother's memory." The General's sister, The Princess Cantacuzene, was married to the Naval Aide to Czar Nicholas of All the Russias. In 1971, at the age of ninety-five, she invited Chase and me to dine with her at her home in Washington on Thanksgiving Day. Since my mother was visiting us from Thomasville at that time, she was included in the invitation. During the meal, the Princess related stories of how, in 1917, she and the Prince had put their children on a barge in the Volga River with instructions to meet at the home of a relative in San Francisco whenever they could all reunite. She and the Prince walked out of Russia and escaped the massacres that were taking place. (The family was not united for eighteen months.) I learned more Russian History during that meal than I had learned at West Point or during subsequent graduate courses. The General died at age eighty-seven, but the Princess lived to be ninety-nine.

Another member of the West Point Society in Washington, DC, was Lieutenant General Leslie R. Groves, the Director of The Manhattan Project which planned, coordinated and carried out the activities associated with the first atomic bomb. In the inscription which he wrote in my copy of his book, Now It Can Be Told, General Groves penned "With my very best wishes to Bill Raiford....I am afraid you won't find this as

...(intriguing) as (Stephane Groueff's) <u>The Manhattan Project</u>. I had to be discrete." The book is fascinating.

In 1976, the Congress of the United States passed a law requiring each of the Service Academies to admit women. Shortly after the passage of that law, Chase and I had the pleasure to dine at the home of friends in Washington, the host having retired from the CIA and the guests of honor were Senator and Mrs. Barry M. Goldwater, also friends of the host and hostess. During coffee and liqueurs in the library, Senator Goldwater said to me, "Bill, I want you to know that I was so incensed over that bill that I tried to attach a rider to the Appropriations Bill, requiring every candidate for admission to West Point to be required to piss over a six-foot fence standing flat-footed." His wife, Peggy, leaned over to her husband and said, "And that's the reason you're not the President today."

Over the period from 1966 until 1997, while I was in Washington, DC, I served at various times on the Board of Admissions and the Board of Governors of the University Club; Sergeant-at-Arms and Director of the Rotary Club; Chairman of the Finance Committee and Director of The Army and Navy Club; and Chairman of the Washington Chamber Orchestra. In 1976, I was elected to membership in The Cosmos Club with the designation "Distinguished Pianist and Composer." I also served as a Member of both the Music and Nominating Committees, as Chairman of the Cosmos Endowment Committee, and as a Member of the Board of Management. The Cosmos Club is the only organization in the world where membership is recommended solely on accomplishments.

From 1965 until 1970, I visited Walter Reed Army Hospital weekly, taking a spinet piano on rollers to the various wards where the wounded from the Vietnam War were recuperating, and playing requests for the men. On several occasions during the first year, I was assisted by Mr. Willard Scott, the original "Ronald McDonald", who was always dressed in his clown costume. Willard later became the noted TV Weatherman.

About twenty years before he became the President of the French Republic, Jacques Chirac was elected the Mayor of Paris. As such, he was invited to attend a luncheon in Washington, DC, hosted by the Center for Strategic and International Studies (CSIS), and by its Chairman, Ambassador David M. Abshire. David and I had been at West Point at the same time. He was a member of the Class of 1951; and I, 1952. (David had recently been the United States Ambassador to NATO.) David invited me to attend the luncheon and to sit at the head (circular) table with his honored guest. During the meal, I asked the Mayor if this was his first visit to the United States. "No", replied Chirac. "When I was in my mid-twenties, I came to New York City and hitchhiked across the United States to San Francisco. I read in the San Francisco 'Chronicle' an advertisement seeking a driver for a lady who wanted to be driven from San Francisco to Dallas. I applied for and got the job." "Did you have a nice trip?", I asked. With a right hand gesture that resembled one playing air guitar, and a guttural sound of delight, the Mayor indicated that he had had a very pleasant trip.

During my lifetime, I have been hospitalized only three times for surgery. The first time was in 1935 in Thomasville for a T&A (Tonsillectomy and Adenoidectomy) at Archbold. I remember so well my Nurse, Miss Prince, for she kept me well supplied with ice cream.

My second hospitalization occurred in 1991 at the Georgetown University Hospital in Washington, DC. I had gone to my Internist for my annual physical checkup, when he discovered, on my chest x-ray, a spot which he did not like. A second x-ray confirmed that I had a calcified aneurysm on the aorta at the juncture with the spine. He told me that it had probably been there for twenty to thirty years and would probably not cause me any problems. However, he said, "If the aneurysm should rupture, you are a dead duck." Without further adieu, the surgery was performed a few days later. I was warned that this surgery was one of the most severe and painful ones a man could have, and that I should plan to be in the hospital for about ten days, followed by several weeks recuperation at home. On the third day after my surgery, the drainage tubes were removed and I was transferred to a "step down" room. On the fourth day, my Surgeon informed me that my healing process had been so rapid that I could go home "in the morning." To make this dissertation short, I am pleased to report that four weeks after my surgery, I was back at my desk at the office. And ten weeks after the surgery, I was lifting weights again!

The third hospitalization was in 1996. On a Sunday morning, as I was taking my shower, I felt a numbness in my left arm. I recognized one of the symptoms of a heart attack, so Chase drove me to the Bethesda (Maryland) Hospital. On the way to the hospital, in the car, I became nauseous. Upon arrival at the Emergency Room, I was immediately placed on a gurney and hooked up to the appropriate machines. Within a few minutes, I experienced a second attack which, fortunately, was observed and recorded by the machines. Later that morning, the Doctor informed me that both attacks had been relatively minor and that it appeared that no major damage had been done. I was transferred to the Washington Hospital Center in the District of Columbia where an MRI was performed. It was determined that only one of my arteries near my heart appeared to have any blockage at all, but that it was about a ninety per cent stoppage. A stent was then inserted and, after two days, I was sent home. I have not had any further problems with my heart or any subsequent health problems. I continue to swim each morning at the Y.M.C.A in Thomasville and watch my diet closely. I enjoy cooking and do so often. I enjoy entertaining and have from three to seven guests at my table, usually monthly. Life is good. I have tried to follow the instructions given to Orson Welles by his physician, that he should discontinue his dinners for four when there is no one else present.

In 1981, it appeared that I had "matured" enough in the eyes of some to strike out on my own, so to speak. I was assisted in forming an investment company, Asset Management International (AMI), and at the same time, I officially became an Advisor to the Defense Intelligence Agency (DIA) on Middle Eastern Affairs. My Board of Directors of AMI consisted of the immediate past President of Bank Melli, headquartered in Teheran, Iran; a Director of the Export-Import Bank of the United States; a past employee of a major stock brokerage firm who had been manager of that firm's branches in Havana, Rio de Janeiro, Caracas, Santiago, and Madrid, and who was also a former FBI Agent; and the Founder and Chairman of a major Internet Service firm. My objectives in forming the Company were to secure significant accounts for the purpose of portfolio management and to establish relationships in major areas of the world where my talents in money management and a proficiency in languages could be utilized. At the same time, I also continued with my piano performances. My "new" life was now taking on an entirely different aspect.

My first trip abroad shortly after the formation of my company was to the Persian Gulf region, specifically to the United Arab Emirates, Kuwait, Bahrain and other "ports of call." Through the assistance and contacts of my Board members, I was able to meet quite a few individuals who were able to "use my services." One of my past experiences was quite helpful in this regard. Several years before my Company was formed, I was elected to membership on the Board of Directors of The First American Bank of Maryland, a component Bank of Financial General, which later became known as The International Bank of Washington, DC. The United States Congress had approved the creation of this entity, with Mr. Clark Clifford (former Military Aide to President Truman and former Secretary of Defense in the Administration of President Johnson) serving as its Chairman, and United States Senator Stuart Symington of Missouri as its Vice-Chairman. The owners of the Bank were Sheikh Zayed, Emir of the United Arab Emirates and of Abu Dhabi, one of the Emirates; the Chief of Saudi Arabian Intelligence; and the Chief of Security for the State of Kuwait. Congress' approval of this arrangement hinged on the absolute understanding that all power of daily control was vested in the Chairman and Vice Chairman, and that not one of the three owners of the Bank had any authority or say-so in the operations of the Bank. On each of my several visits to this region of the world, Mr. Clifford would brief me on my assignment. The discussion went something like this: "Now, Bill, please remind Sheikh Zayed that you are there looking for investment counsel business for your company, and not as a member of the Board of the Bank he owns."

One of the most interesting persons I have ever met from the Middle East was Mehdi Fakharzadeh, an Iranian who came to America in the 1950s. Having no knowledge of the insurance industry, he convinced the Metropolitan Life Insurance Company to give him a job and train him in the industry. He became the first insurance salesman in the world to "write" a policy for $1,000,000 on an individual. After Mehdi and I became friends, he passed on to me some "pearls of Iranian wisdom." They have stood me in good stead in my professional life and particularly on my visits to the Middle East. Here are just two of them:

"Do not be quick to speak when you are not asked to do so."

"Do not measure the cloth before you have settled on the price."

In the early 1980s, on one of my visits to the State of Kuwait, my visit coincided with the meeting in Kuwait of the Organization of Petroleum Exporting Countries (OPEC). When I checked into my hotel, which just happened to be the headquarters of the OPEC conferees, I was greeted in the lobby with a scene the likes of which I had never before encountered. At a table in the lobby on which a sub-machine gun was situated, there were two armed men in the uniforms of the Kuwaiti Army, with a bandoleer of ammunition across each shoulder. My VISA said "TOURIST" and the explanation thereon was "Investment Counselor prospecting for business." Without any difficulty, I completed my check-in and proceeded to the elevator, where I found another armed Kuwaiti soldier. Stepping off on my assigned floor, I found two additional armed Kuwaiti soldiers patrolling the hall. My first reaction was "agonies of enjoyment": I could not fail to feel securely guarded while at the same time I experienced a feeling of total fear. To calm my nerves, I changed into my swim suit and robe and proceeded to the pool where there were several other men, but no females. When I chose a lounge chair and stretched out for some sun, the man next to me began to comment on the armed personnel in the hotel. We introduced ourselves. He indicated that he was a pharmaceutical representative from London calling on the Kuwaiti State Hospital. I could not fail to observe that he appeared more like a professional body builder and karate expert than a pharmaceutical salesman. After several more minutes of back and forth conversation, we mutually agreed not to ask any more questions. In about one hour, he got up to leave the pool and I never saw him again during my stay. Later that same day, I received a telephone call from the secretary of the gentleman with whom I had an appointment the next day. The secretary indicated that a car would pick me up in front of the hotel at ten o'clock the next morning.

At five of ten, I arrived downstairs and noticed that the guards were still in place in the lobby. When I walked outside the hotel, a black limousine with tinted window glass was awaiting me. The driver, a young Kuwaiti of about twenty-five years, called me by name as he opened the right rear door. I got in. The drive to the building where my appointment was scheduled was only about ten blocks from the hotel. As we arrived at the building and proceeded down the ramp to an underground parking spot, the driver again opened the door for me and accompanied me to the elevator, which he boarded with me for our ascent to the penthouse. As the elevator door opened, I found myself in a very expansive lobby with a magnificent view of all of Kuwait City. The male receptionist immediately ushered me into the private office of my potential new investment client. Upon being shown a seat, a young man arrived with coffee served in small cups. I was aware that the Kuwaiti coffee was strong, but "strong" did not adequately describe the contents of my cup. I was also aware of the custom in the Arab world that one may accept a second cup of the proffered beverage, but if it be taken, one is required to take a third. Even numbers of cups are considered gauche and definitely unacceptable in polite society. As I finished my first and only cup, and had established my credentials, eight young men with note pads and pens arrived and seated themselves in a semicircle at the rear of the room. My potential client explained that he always had eight secretaries for each conversation with a visitor, "to insure that I fully understand everything that was discussed." I was once again feeling my "agonies of enjoyment", for I was not quite sure how far I should proceed in our conversation. It is an established fact in the Arab World that no one discusses his financial situation in the presence of anyone else. After a few minutes, my host, sensing my uneasiness with the situation, dismissed the eight men. After they had left the room, he explained that it was an established procedure in his office to have the men present whenever there were guests, and that eyebrows might be raised if he did not follow that procedure. He suggested that he accompany me back to the hotel. When we got back in the limousine, he introduced me to the driver, his oldest son, and assured me that our conversation would be totally confidential. I relaxed as we drove back to the hotel, the ten-block drive taking about one hour.

Visiting the old souk in Kuwait City was a marvelous and interesting experience. The souk, sometimes spelled "suk", is the local trading post where a varied assortment of merchants gather daily to smoke their hookahs and trade their wares, to each other or to the public at large. The gold merchants walk around with their arms laden with gold bracelets, their necks adorned with gold necklaces and their fingers crammed interstitially with U.S. one hundred dollar bills. The rug merchants lay their rugs on the ground and everyone and every camel seemed to have traversed them before I got there. All transactions are done in cash (no credit cards!) and the price of each article is always rounded to the next one hundred dollars, which seemed to be the standard unit of exchange. I made several purchases at the souk on my visits to Kuwait, but I did not ever buy a camel. It would not fit into my luggage!

One of our former United States Ambassadors to Kuwait was also quite a good artist. His paintings and prints were in demand. One of his oils is a depiction of a door of an old building in Kuwait City. He had several prints of this work made to be used as gifts. I am fortunate to have received an autographed print in 1983, which now hangs on the wall of my "I like me" room. This print is of significance, for it was at this door that I occasionally met one of the "beggars" who always had something of interest to tell (sell) me.

On one of my visits to the Persian Gulf, after having made several trips thereto, I was met at the airport by the same young friend I had met in Washington years before at a social function at the Embassy of his Country. He was a nephew of the Emir, and was a talented and delightful young man. On this particular visit, he met me in his newest car, and, as we drove into the city, he said, "Tonight we are dining at a new restaurant I think you will like." As we drove up to a nondescript building with no indication of its purpose or use, we exited from the automobile and entered a beautifully decorated Italian ambiance. There was only one table and it was in the center of the dining room. However, there were twenty-four liveried waiters in white gloves standing at attention and awaiting our beck and call. The evening was spent enjoying a magnificent Italian cuisine in a wonderfully hushed atmosphere of complete security.

On another visit to one of the Emirates, the American Ambassador to the Emirates honored me by hosting a musicale and reception, with me as the featured pianist for the evening. He had even imported a Steinway grand piano for the occasion. Invitees were all the Ambassadors accredited to the Emirates. I played an all-Chopin program. During the reception that followed, the Ambassador from another mid-Eastern country complimented me on my performance and added that he had not heard such beautiful music since he had arrived "in this God-forsaken country." The evening was a huge success, as I was able to make several new friends and contacts.

One of my favorite places to walk in the evenings was along the concrete "boardwalk" on the Persian Gulf in Abu Dhabi. This is known as the "Corniche", which is the French word for a "ledge." Parts of it really do extend out over the water. Every hundred feet or so there is a lamp post with a hanging circular basket containing flowers which are watered each evening after sundown by a watering truck containing distilled water. Between every two lamp posts is a bench. Although it is a popular promenade for families in the early evening, about ten or eleven o'clock it becomes more sparsely inhabited and provides a fine place for rendezvous. Some of my best exchanges of ideas have occurred on the Corniche.

On another of my visits to the Gulf, I met with a friend of a friend in Bahrain, who just happened to be a member of the Royal family. He also was an accomplished pianist and was a classmate at Sandhurst of my friend in Bahrain. Small world! Being a graduate of West Point, I was able to talk about his days at Sandhurst, and being a pianist also, we were able to establish very good and cordial relations. And, as a member of the Royal family, no one nor no thing was out of his reach. He opened many doors for me and introduced me to many new friends and contacts. On a subsequent occasion, we were able to meet in London and enjoy a delightful evening together. Unfortunately, he suffered a fatal heart attack in the mid 90s.

On another proposed trip to the Island State of Bahrain in the Persian Gulf, I planned to visit the aluminum processing plant on the Island. I knew that it was the largest aluminum processing plant in the world, but I had very few details about its operations. One of my partners in my Company, AMI, had discovered that the Personnel Retirement and Pension Plans of the Aluminum Company were being managed by a major brokerage house in the U.S. Through a West Point friend who was currently the Director of the Aluminum Institute in Washington, DC, I was able to get an appointment with the Manager of the Pension and Retirement Plans for that Company. The purpose of my visit was to present the capabilities of my Company, AMI, in the area of Money Management, and to make a "pitch" for the possibility of taking over some of the assets in the Plans, or to get the entire Plan away from its current managers. When I met with the Company's Plan Manager in his office within the plant, I made my presentation on Money Management and the capabilities of our firm, and showed him a partial list of clients currently doing business with us. All the clients on my list had been previously contacted and had agreed to having their names disclosed. The Plan Manager listened intently and then informed me that he would have to present my Money Management "pitch" to the entire Board of Directors, for their consideration. I thanked him for his courtesies to me; and then I brought up the idea that, if I be successful in "getting the business", it would be very helpful to me and to my firm if we knew some details of the personnel who were participants in the Plans. Also it would be educational if I knew more about the Plant itself and its operations. The Plan Manager agreed that this might be helpful and began to give me documents, pictures, charts, production schedules, bauxite ore input and aluminum ingot output. When I departed the Plant, my brief case was bulging with documentation. Although I was never able to secure the management of the Plan's assets, I did meet several interesting people as a result of that visit and gained much valuable information on the largest aluminum processing plant in the world.

On each of my many visits to the different areas of the Middle East, I took special note of the fact that women took no part in the business affairs of the region. While women are now making some headway in some of the countries of the Middle East; particularly in Dubai, one of the Emirates on the Persian Gulf, where women are being taught English in the University; the vast majority of the countries throughout the Arab World still do not allow women to participate in any of their business functions. In every conversation that I had with any official back in the

States, I strongly suggested that my Government pay particular attention to this fact. In the many contacts and meetings I had in the Arab World during my twenty-plus years of service there, no women were ever present. In addition, when I was invited to dine in the home of a friend or a new contact; upon arrival, I was introduced to the wife and daughters, if there be any, but all females would then retire to another part of the house and did not share in the meal with the men.

After the Iraqi invasion of Kuwait and the subsequent withdrawal of all troops, the United States Administration in power appointed a woman Ambassador to Iraq. This was an effrontery, not only to Iraq, but also to the entire Arab World; and it sent a strong message that the United States either did not understand Arab culture or was deliberately attempting to show its superiority and arrogance. While in later years there have been several women appointed to positions of authority in some of the Arab countries, the actions of the United States Administration at that time in that country was not viewed favorably. In my opinion, no progress will ever be made in diplomacy between the United States and the Arab countries until this country realizes and acknowledges that it understands and accepts the social customs and traditions of the other party. We must never take a second cup of coffee and refuse a third.

<hr>

I would now like to comment on a visit to Moscow in 1975. The weather on this particular visit was abominable. The noontime temperature was 105 degrees Fahrenheit. And it was May! I had had several meetings with friends of friends, and decided one afternoon to take a stroll through Gorky Park. I sat down on a bench to rest, when a young man dressed in athletic attire and running shoes sat down on the other end of my bench. After a very long silence, he asked, in hushed and broken English, if I were an American. When I replied in the affirmative, he indicated that he wanted to speak in English but that we should not be seen talking together. He told me that he was an athlete from Ukraine and that he was in Moscow for a track meet, but that no facilities had been provided for the athletes, no accommodations, no food, no nothing. He suggested that we walk, not together, but in a column, like ducks! I would speak over my shoulder and he would reply. We walked for about an hour. Then we came upon a food shop where I bought him something to eat and drink. After that, we said good bye. I have always wondered what happened to him.

Moscow was a fascinating place in the 1970s. One evening, I visited the Hotel Metropole for dinner. The dining room decor was red velvet and palm trees, circa 1890. When my young waiter arrived at my table and I had greeted him in Russian, he responded that he spoke very good English, having studied at the University of Pittsburgh! So we conversed the entire evening, I in Russian and he in English. We must have sounded to our neighboring tables like a sidewalk café at the U.N.

When I arrived in Moscow the first time, I proceeded to Customs to be cleared. I had nothing in my baggage that would appear to be "subversive" or that should have delayed me. However, I had purchased a copy of "Time" magazine in the London Airport. On the cover of that particular issue was the photograph of a couple of young Russian ballet dancers who had defected to the United States. The Customs agent confiscated my magazine; and, while I stood there waiting for my clearance, the agent proceeded to "read" that issue of "Time", from cover to cover.

This took approximately two hours! When he finally decided to give me a clearance, I was gently but forcibly put into a cab and transported to my hotel, ironically named the Hotel Intourist. When I arrived in the lobby, I was given my room key. It was a key attached to a rather pendulous, four-inch, bell-shaped "gizmo" that, when inverted in the key board of the hotel desk, made an electronic contact and indicated that the room's occupant had left the hotel, allowing the hotel personnel to clean and, I am sure, search the room. A guest was not allowed to leave the lobby for the outside without having deposited his room key at the desk. My room contained a bunk bed with a straw mattress and a chest of drawers and a chair. The bathroom was a normal one but there was no soap. And so to bed.

When I awakened and went to the lobby for my breakfast, I noticed a young man standing near a post, staring at me as I proceeded through the lobby to the dining room. When I returned to the lobby, this same young man approached me and said that he had been assigned to be my guide while I was in Moscow. I asked if it were usual for guests to have guides, and was assured that it was the normal custom. On the first day with my guide, I visited every museum I could find. I visited Lenin's Tomb. I visited the GUM Department Store. I visited Saint Basil's Cathedral and the Kremlin. By nightfall, we were both very tired when I left my "guide" in the lobby. I suggested that I would like to begin the following morning about 6 A.M. and spend the entire day walking over as much of Moscow as I could cover in one day. At about four in the afternoon, I suggested that we stop for some tea. He readily agreed. Over a glass of hot Russian tea, I discovered that he was studying The American Constitution for his Master's Degree at the University of Moscow. He knew more about the writings of James Madison than I did! He had been a "tour guide" for about one year. When we got to know each other, we found out that we liked each other. I told him that I would be flying to Kiev the next evening for a two-day stay. He said that he had business in Kiev and would see me there. When I arrived at the Moscow airport for my 10 o'clock flight, I discovered that it was delayed two hours - no reason given. I assumed that the night flight meant no observation of the ground from the air. When I arrived at the airport in Kiev, there stood my "tour guide." All in all, we spent six days together and I became very fond of this young man and felt that he had much potential for the future. When I got back to Washington, DC, I had an occasion to be at the Embassy of the Soviet Socialist Republics for a cocktail buffet, at which time I engaged the Soviet Ambassador, Anatoly Dobrinyin, in conversation. I told the Ambassador of my recent trip to the Soviet Union and of meeting my "tour guide." I also told the Ambassador that I thought that this young man had great potential and that he would fit very well into the Diplomatic Service. About two years later, I received a letter from my "tour guide" informing me that he was now in training in the Diplomatic School in Moscow; and that he had hopes of becoming, at least, an Attaché. I am pleased to report that this same young man became the Ambassador to an Eastern Country, served there for three years and was then made Ambassador of his home Republic to a most prestigious post in the Third World. Over the years, we have kept in contact, sharing pictures, books and Christmas cards. He is married and has one daughter.

On another occasion in Moscow, I went to the Bolshoi Theatre to see if there might be one ticket for the evening's performance. When I was told that it was a sellout, I informed the ticket agent that I was going back to my hotel room and would await the possibility of a cancellation. I left with him the full amount of the ticket, plus a gratuity, and returned to my hotel. I had been in the room less than ten minutes when I received a call informing me that there had been a cancellation and my ticket would be held at the box office for me. I arrived at the theatre a few minutes before the beginning of the performance and took my seat. Just prior to the rise of the curtain, a young lady eased into the vacant seat beside me. At intermission, the two of us began to speak, in English. In the vestibule, I bought two glasses of champagne for us and asked about her life. She informed me that she was an American "from Pittsburgh" and was just visiting in Moscow. I inquired if, after the performance, she would like to have dinner with me. When she replied that she would be unable to do so because she had an early morning appointment and had to "wash my hair come high hell or water", I knew that she was a "plant." Her questions to me during our conversations were very pointed, though they elicited nothing of importance in response. Parenthetically, I might add that it appeared that everyone I met "by chance" was from Pittsburgh!

One morning as I came down to the lobby of my hotel, I noticed a group of American women standing around, seemingly awaiting transportation. "William Raiford", shouted one of the ladies. She was a cousin of my father from Pavo, Georgia. After the requisite snapshots, they went on their tour. Unfortunately, we never saw each other again in Moscow.

On a visit to Kiev in Ukraine, I was impressed with the cleanliness of the city and the magnitude of the music emanating from many of the building's open windows. I visited a rather large music store near the Tschaikovsky Conservatory and, with permission, played a few selections on a grand piano, drawing a rather large audience. This pleased me very much and quickly made up for the previous night when I had arrived at my assigned hotel to find that no reservation was on the books. I had to wait approximately two hours until a place could be found for me to sleep. It turned out to be a cot in the ballroom!

When I left Moscow, a Russian friend told me that I was the only American that he knew who spoke with a Southern Russian accent. I told him that I was from Georgia, but that went directly over his head! Punning is not a Russian trait.

One of the items in my collection of inscribed books is the three volume set of the <u>Gulag Archipeligo</u>, printed in Paris in the Russian language and inscribed in volume one as follows: "For William Raiford. Sept. 1989, (Alexandre) Solzhenitsyn", all in the Cyrillic alphabet. The introduction was made by Mstislav (Slava) Rostropovich, Conductor of the Washington National Symphony and a friend of many years.

📖 📖 📖

Chase and I had an enjoyable trip to London one Spring with a side trip to the Cotswold. We stayed at The Ligon Arms in Broadway, a remarkably preserved hotel which was the residence of Oliver Cromwell during the Interregnum. Visiting Chipping Camden and Warwick Castle was interesting, but I would never have survived residence in such a drafty place as the castle. We shopped in London, which I discovered was Chase's favorite city in Europe. We tried to see the Queen but she was not in residence!

Once I spent an interesting week on the Costa del Sol in Southern Spain. An acquaintance of mine happened to own a villa that literally hung out over the Mediterranean Sea near the town of Marbella. Having a glass of wine with him at sunset on his deck, I asked who were his neighbors. "Elizabeth and Philip own that one on the right", he said, pointing, "and a very famous actor owns that one on the left." Of course, I thought he was pulling my leg, and I said so. "Look to your left", he said, and there on his patio was the actor named. We all exchanged waves, but I never did see the Queen or Philip!

When I left Marbella, I drove down the Coast to Gibralter and to the port town of Algeciras, from where I took a hydroplane over to Africa and the city of Tangier. One of the must-do tourist attractions was to ride a camel, which I did, complete with a red fez. When I later showed that photograph to my wife, she opined that the camel did not look as though he was enjoying the ride. I had always heard that if you thought yourself to be a linguist, go to the Bazaar in Tangier. There, it was alleged that any language and any dialect would be understood by someone. I decided to purchase a piece of pottery for our home in Maryland, so I wandered to the pottery section of the Bazaar, where I was approached by a nicely dressed young man who appeared to be about twenty-five years of age. His nationality was indeterminate. So having just left Spain after a week's visit, I decided to speak to this young man in Spanish. His responses were perfect in the Castilian dialect. I then switched into the French language and was further amazed to hear flawless French. I'll get him, I thought as I began conversing with him in the Russian language. His responses in the Moscovian dialect completely convinced me that what I had heard about the Bazaar was in fact true. So finally, I said in English, "Your knowledge of languages is superb." To which he replied in the most beautiful Oxfordian I had ever heard, "Thank you 'veddy' much." I responded with, "And your English is beautiful." "Thank you a-gain", came the reply, "and I thought we would never get there." I bought the pottery.

Before I left Tangier, I drove to the residence of Barbara Hutton and was impressed to note that her home was larger than that of the Prince of Morocco.

📖 📖 📖

In 1981, I had the pleasure to attend the International Gold Conference in London. There were approximately seven hundred attendees from all over the world. At the final session, the moderator asked for a show of hands as to how many of us thought that the price of gold would rise to $1,000. per ounce in the near future. (The price of gold at that time was slightly over $800. per ounce.) Approximately one half of the audience put up their hands. He then asked how many thought that the price of gold would fall to $400. per ounce in the near future. The hands of the other half of the audience went up. Even the so-called experts were about equally divided! Upon my return to the States, I had the opportunity to report on my findings from the Conference to some friends fairly high up in the Administration. I boldly declared, that since the assets and the net worth of the United States no longer depended on our gold reserves, we should announce to the world that we were selling all our gold on the open market, with the proviso that we would never again buy it back at any price. I further suggested that the proceeds from the sales should be applied to reducing the National debt. To date, no action has been taken on these suggestions!

During an earlier Administration, I had the opportunity to offer some thoughts on the debt situation confronting the United States and all our foreign debtors. Perhaps at the time, it appeared revolutionary, but I suggested that the United States do three things simultaneously: (1) Abolish the World Bank, (2) Abolish the International Monetary Fund, and (3) Cancel the debts of all debtor countries to the United States with the understanding that we would never again lend any amount to anyone. I felt, as I still do, that countries need to stand on their own, not to be beholden to any other country, and not to be burdened, psychologically as well as factually, with a debt that they can never nor will they ever repay. I find it interesting to note that, by 2006, the debts of quite a few African nations had been cancelled.

In December of 1980, I was called one day at my office in Washington by Central Casting of DC, asking me if I would be interested in trying out for a part in a movie to be filmed in the District. At the time, I had a full beard. When I was interviewed, I was selected to play the part of a United States Senator. The movie to be filmed was "Reds", directed by Warren Beatty. Although I had several scenes with speaking parts, the final cut eliminated all my speaking parts but left me in two scenes, one exiting from the Old State Department Building next to The White House, and the other descending the steps of the United States Senate on Capitol Hill. It was interesting working with Warren Beatty, for which I received an inscribed picture of the two of us, me in costume, warming by an open fire in a barrel, on the grounds of the park behind The White House. When "Reds" was released in 1981, it won the

Academy Award for Best Picture of the year. I feel certain that my acting was a contributing factor! Chase asked me, after the Awards Ceremony, what I planned to do for an encore. It was not until 1990 that my "acting career" was again challenged. The movie was "The Bonfire of the Vanities" with Tom Hanks, Bruce Willis and Melanie Griffith. I had only one scene and my selection was due to the fact that a friend at The United Nations in New York City was a friend of the Director, Brian De Palma. In the final scene, when Bruce Willis is receiving his latest accolade for the book he has written about the subject of the movie, there is a dinner in The Palm Court of the World Trade Building in New York City with about four hundred "extras", all in tuxedos and long dresses, cheering the awardee. I am seated in the first row of tables, nearest the dais, at the center table, facing the camera. Although the movie did not receive favorable reviews, I can only wonder that it might have had a greater impact if I had had a speaking part! In his inscription in my copy of his book, Tom Wolfe has written, "To Bill Raiford of God's country." Tom is very fond of South Georgia, especially the area from Albany to Thomasville, as was demonstrated in his later book, A Man in Full.

In 1985, I was invited to join the firm of E.F. Hutton, taking all my accounts with me. Since that time until my retirement in 2001, my office remained at the same location. The only thing that changed was the name of the company for whom I worked. Over that sixteen-year period, there were names such as E.F. Hutton, Shearson, Lehman, American Express, Solomon, Smith Barney, and various combinations thereof. The joke around the office was: If my boss calls, get his name! In 1988,

I was designated a Senior Portfolio Manager by Shearson Lehman Hutton and honored by the firm as one of the Top Ten Performers in the Nation.

In 1986, I was inducted as a Chevalier de La Confrérie des Chevaliers du Tastevin. This is the International Burgundy Wine Society. In 1991, I was elevated to the rank of Commandeur. On my first visit to the Château du Clos de Vougeot, the seat of the Confrérie, built in 1550 and located in the Côte d'Or, between Dijon on the northern end and Beaune on the southern end; I was "housed" in the Hôtel de la Cloche in Dijon. On the evening of the "black tie" dinner, I was picked up by a driver and we arrived at the Château at about six o'clock. A champagne reception was held in the courtyard of the Château. At seven o'clock, all five hundred guests were directed down the sandstone steps to the dining hall on the underground level. In attendance that evening were members of the Confrérie from the United States, France, Italy, Germany, Poland and Japan and their spouses. During the five course dinner, each course accompanied by a different wine of Burgundy, the "Cadets de Bourgogne" sang and entertained the guests with questions and answers in the six languages represented that evening. While I did not speak all the languages being used, after a few hours of hearing the patter, I was able to discern the gist of the humor. At the completion of the evening's entertainment, I was driven back to my hotel in Dijon. What a grand experience!

At a dinner party in Paris, to which I had been invited by a friend of the host, the conversation suddenly turned to the miserable state of affairs which had resulted because of the election of the Socialist President Mitterand. It was miserable to some of the wealthy and more vocal attendees because of the prohibition, dictated by the new Government, from sending any capital out of France. I asked the well-known owner of some of the most famous vineyards in France how this prohibition was going to effect him. "My dear fellow", he replied, "My vineyards have been in Switzerland for thirty years." What a magnificent bit of prior planning, I thought! After we had left the table and were seated for liqueurs in the rather large drawing room which had three or four conversation pits; my host, my friend and I began talking in earnest about the flow of capital in Europe. My host asked me if I had noticed the painting hanging over the credenza in his dining room. When I identified it as one of the paintings of Jacques Louis David not hanging in a major museum, my host asked, rather bluntly, if I could assist him in getting the painting to America. His question included the offer of a substantial commission if I were to be successful. Using every ounce of diplomacy at my discretion, I thanked him for considering me for such a task, but had to decline since the painting would require an exit Visa issued by the Louvre and approved by the French Government. I knew, by the question, that he was implying an exit by other means; but I refused to take the bait. After we left the home of our host, I said to my friend that I believed the offer was made in all seriousness. He assured me that it was.

📖 📖 📖

In 1986, for our thirtieth wedding anniversary, Chase and I flew from New York to Oslo, Norway, where we boarded the French liner, Mermoz, and transited the Baltic Sea at night. During the eight-day trip and during the daytime, we debarked in Copenhagen, Denmark, and Stockholm, Sweden, and ended the cruise in Helsinki, Finland, from whence we flew back to New York. On one occasion, while we were shopping in Stockholm, Chase and I met on the street a friend and client of mine who at that time was living in Hong Kong. He just happened to be in the city on business. Also, while in Stockholm, we were invited to a cocktail party aboard the yacht of Barbara Hutton, whose father had founded E.F. Hutton, the firm I had joined the previous year.

In 1988, Chase an I made our semi-annual visit to Thomasville for the celebration of my mother's 90th birthday. During our visit, I inquired on a Saturday morning whether or not mother might like to go out for lunch. Accepting our invitation, she said "Let me get my hat and gloves." I told her that we were only going to her favorite eatery, The Golden Corral, and that a hat and gloves would not be required. She looked at me as though I had lost my mind and forgotten all my "upbringing." "Ladies", she said "don't go out of the house without their hat and gloves." She proceeded to put on the white gloves she had crocheted with the butcher's string from my father's store, and a hat that she had "re-styled" herself. I then remembered that she had worked at Neel's Department Store in Thomasville before she was married in 1918 and had been a close friend and co-worker of Mrs. Essie Baker. I feel certain that she had gotten some important millinery ideas from Miss Essie.

After my parents were divorced in 1950, my mother, at age fifty-two, began training as a Practical Nurse. After her graduation and "capping", she worked at the Vereen Memorial Hospital in Moultrie, Georgia; at the Presbyterian Children's Home in Talladega, Alabama; and finally at Archbold Memorial Hospital in Thomasville, under the supervision of the Head Nurse, Miss Lillian Presnell. It was obvious that mother was a good nurse and was well-liked, because Miss Presnell allowed her to continue her services until the age of seventy. After retiring from her regular duties at Archbold, she continued for a few years in private duty with patients she had previously worked with at the hospital.

On the occasion of her ninetieth birthday, she sent to both of her children a quatrain which she had composed. It goes like this:

> I can live with my arthritis,
> My false teeth fit jes' fine.
> I can see through my bifocals,
> But I sho' do miss my mind!

At the age of ninety-two, in 1990, mother decided that she should give up driving her 1963 Chevrolet, (with less than 35,000 miles!) and move from her apartment on Broad Street into an assisted living facility farther out Broad Street, where she remained the rest of her life. Ten days before her death, she had a stroke and lapsed into a coma. However, two days before her death, she awoke and asked the nurse on duty what day it was. When told, she said "I will be ninety-seven on Friday." On the 19th of May, 1995, on her ninety-seventh birthday, she died in her sleep.

In the Fall of 1988, I was asked by the Superintendent of the United States Military Academy, Lieutenant General Dave Palmer, West Point

Class of 1956; and the President of the Association of Graduates of West Point, General Michael Davison, West Point Class of 1939, to accept the position of Chairman of West Point's Bicentennial Steering Group (BSG), a group charged with the planning and the coordination of the 200th Birthday celebrations of the Academy, in 2002. When I told Chase that I had accepted this fourteen-year assignment, she indicated that she thought I had lost my mind! However, the many and varied tasks and events which were conceived, thoroughly discussed and finally agreed upon for implementation were assigned to one or more of several Committees, headed by senior graduates of West Point or persons of equal or higher rank in their civilian fields. Included in the events which finally took place were the issuances of a silver dollar and a postage stamp, both on the same date, 16 March 2002. It was the first time in the history of the United States that a coin and a stamp had been issued on the same date for the same institution. Also, on that date, there was a concert in Carnegie Hall similar to the one which took place in 1952, in which the United States Military Academy Band and the West Point Glee Club performed, assisted by Mr. Walter Cronkite, who conducted one March with the Band. Walter had been a friend of West Point for many decades and when asked to participate in our Bicentennial, he readily agreed. As an aside, I might add that Walter's great-great-grandmother was named "Renz" and my wife's great-great-great-grandmother was also named "Renz." The inscription in his book, <u>A Reporter's Life</u>, in my personal library, reads in part: "To Bill Raiford - Anyone married to a Renz is a friend, and may be a relative of mine." Through the good graces of Jess Jackson, Founder, and Lew Platt, CEO, we were also successful in getting the Kendall-Jackson Winery in California to issue special labels on both a 2000 Chardonnay and a 1998 Cabernet Sauvignon.

There were many performances by the West Point Band throughout the United States, playing several original works especially commissioned for the Bicentennial. An annual Engineering Bridge Design Contest was established, open to all high school students in the United States, with significant prizes and awards attendant thereto. It was recognized and sanctioned by the American Society of Military Engineers. This has become an annual event at West Point and has brought the attention of the Academy to every high school student in America. The culmination of the Bicentennial efforts was the publication of a book, entitled <u>West Point: Two Centuries of Honor and Tradition</u>, edited by Robert Cowley and Thomas Guinzburg and published by Warner Books. This volume contains essays by, among others, Thomas Fleming, Cecilia Holland, Tom Wicker, Arthur Miller, George Plimpton, Stephen Ambrose, David Halberstam, and William F. Buckley, Jr.

The final events of the Bicentennial occurred when the Graduating Class of the French Military Academy at St. Cyr, also founded in 1802, was invited to participate in the Graduation Parade at West Point; and one hundred, twenty Cadets from West Point were invited to march in the Graduation Parade at St. Cyr, a week after the Cadets led the Parade down the Champ Elysées on the French Independence Day, 14 July. This was the first time since 1945 that Americans had paraded in Paris. The Bicentennial of West Point was celebrated in style, but without a lot of "bells and whistles." For my services during the fourteen-year period of planning and executing the events of West Point's Bicentennial Celebration, I was decorated by The Secretary of the Army with the Army Public Service Award.

On 10 November 1988, the West Point Bicentennial Steering Group (BSG) came into being. The Official Order, naming me as the Chairman, was signed by both General Palmer and General Davison. At the very first meeting of our Group, in the Spring of 1989, in one of the rooms in the Headquarters Building at West Point, General Palmer, then the Superintendent at West Point, briefed the Group on our Mission and gave us guidance on how to accomplish it. He also said, as he was leaving the room, that he was having a few guests in for cocktails and dinner at Quarters 100, the residence of the Superintendent and his wife, that evening and that our group of five was invited to join the others. When we arrived about 1830 hours and entered the home, I was once again reminded of a most wonderful (to a true Southerner) fact. Over the mantle in the drawing room on the right, hangs a portrait of Robert E. Lee, West Point Class of 1829, who had served as Superintendent of the Academy in the early 1850s. Over the mantle in the drawing room on the left, hangs a portrait of Sylvanus Thayer, the "Father of the Military Academy" and a graduate of West Point in the Class of 1808. As we five entered the left-hand drawing room, I noticed that General Palmer was in conversation with a most beautiful lady whom I immediately recognized. "Bill," said the General, "I would like to introduce you to the Countess of Romanones." As the Countess extended her hand, she said, "Its all right, Bill, if we know each other here."

My first meeting with the Countess went back several years. In fact, she is the sister-in-law of one of my AMI Board members. Aline Griffith was born in Pearl River, New York. While she was a gorgeous model in New York, she was recruited by the Office of Strategic Services (OSS) to be a spy. After her training, she was flown to Spain. There, in addition to conducting her espionage work, she met and married the Count of Quintanilla, later to become the Count of Romanones. But my story must jump back a few decades more, to the year 1966. World War II had been over for more than twenty years when an ace operative, code name "Tiger," was called out of semi-retirement by the Central Intelligence Agency (CIA), the successor organization to the OSS, for a critical mission: to uncover a highly placed NATO mole who was gravely threatening U.S. security. But "Tiger" is no ordinary spy. She is Aline Griffith, the Countess of Romanones, an internationally prominent socialite who can mix naturally in the right European circles and charm people into saying more than they intend to. To succeed in this assignment, Aline knew that she must recruit a secret partner - a trusted friend whose loyalty is unquestioned and whose social credentials are unsurpassed - a native American susceptible to the pressures of patriotism. Who else but Wallis Simpson, the Duchess of Windsor? In the course of this assignment, Aline and the Duchess were able to search out the Nazi-looted art treasures, discovering that, the closer they got to accomplishing their primary mission, the more they realized that the two missions were intertwined. Aline has written a superb account of this adventure in <u>The Spy Went Dancing</u>, published in 1990 by G.P. Putnam's Sons, and from whose dust jacket I have excerpted some of the previous comments, with the written approval of the authoress. The inscribed copy which I have in my personal library reads, "To that handsome Bill Raiford - - A great West Pointer. Flattered and happy to dance through this with you - - Love, Aline." Incidentally, the code name for the Duchess was "Willy."

The Duke and Duchess of Windsor had been guests in Thomasville at Horseshoe Plantation, the estate of George Baker, on several occasions.

Chase and I lived the majority of our married life of almost forty-five years in the Old Farm Subdivision near Rockville, Maryland. Our three boys attended public schools in Montgomery County, Maryland, which at that time were considered to be one of the most outstanding school systems in the Nation. The boys were good students and superb athletes, basketball being their choice of games. Both Chase and I supervised their education and were active in their extra-curricular activities. Young Bill and Dave also participated in the Boy Scout movement with Bill attaining the rank of Life and Dave achieving that of Eagle.

During the time my three boys were in high school, I was invited by a member of the Montgomery County, Maryland, Judiciary to go with him one night each month to the County Detention Center which was only about one mile from our home. Our purpose in going was to speak to those incarcerated, on a one-on-one basis, on any reasonable subject of their choosing and to let them know that someone cared about their plight and their future. On each visit, I took off my belt and emptied the contents of my pockets before being allowed into the communal area. Each of the separate wards was similarly arranged, with double cubicles opening into the center room which was used as a day room. Each of the cubicles had no door. The population of each ward was about thirty men. The Warden of the Center accompanied us into the ward on our first visit, introduced us and then left the two of us alone with the men. After I had made my fourth visit, I was allowed to continue my visits alone. As the men gathered for our first "session", the variation in dress was noteworthy. Some were dressed in both dungaree shirts and trousers; some were in only trousers; some were in only undershorts. As my visits continued, I began to take note of the fact that the majority of the men were wearing both shirts and trousers. At first, the vocal ones wanted to know what my "agenda" was? Why was I there? They very soon identified me as the father of the three Raiford boys, all of whom played basketball and one of whom was usually mentioned in the "Washington Post" at least once a month. When I identified myself as being "in the financial world", a few of the inmates wanted to show off their knowledge about the markets: gold, oil, stocks, bonds or whatever caught their fancy that evening. On my fifth or sixth visit, I asked if any of them read the Bible. Six or seven admitted that they did and that they prayed daily. I informed them that I was an Associate Sunday School Teacher at the First Baptist Church in downtown Washington and that the other Associate Teacher in our class was President Jimmy Carter. I then pointed out some interesting facts found in the Scriptures, quoted several well-known verses and several less well-known; and then, at the end of our one-hour session, I asked those who desired to do so to stay for a few minutes so we could discuss the possibility of future Bible reading sessions. Five men responded to my invitation. Since we were out of time for that session, I offered to hold a special Bible study session and invited the five to invite any additional cell mates who might be interested to join us. The following month, I held a Bible study group session. Only three men attended at the beginning, but, before the hour was over, two others had joined our group. All the members of this group were already Christians. The two Jewish men in the cell expressed an interest to "listen in." Our group never comprised more than eight, and those eight were constantly changing, since the inmates were either finishing their stint at the Facility and were being released or they were being transferred to the Maryland State Penitentiary. Before each man in "my cell" was scheduled for release to the outside world, I undertook to assist him in finding a job, if he cared for me to do so. Over the three years that I worked in this program, I was able to find jobs for six men, and three of them worked out so well that they were able to operate their own businesses within five years.

I began searching the records of my English ancestry in the early 1970s. I sought out the assistance of The College of Arms in London for I had some information that an early ancestor had come from England to Isle of Wight County, Virginia, in 1679. Through the help I received from The College, I was able to prove that my emigrant ancestor, Philip Raiford, the only Raiford to come to America, had in fact arrived in Virginia in 1679, having sailed from Devonshire in southwestern England. I further was able to establish that he and his sister, Elizabeth, were the only brother and sister Raifords living in all of England in the late 17th Century for whom there did not exist any death or burial records in England. The College also spent much time and effort researching the Raiford Coat-of-Arms, which had been granted during the reign of King Henry II. The Coat appears in the First Edition of Burke's "Landed Gentry", but does not appear in any subsequent edition. The College determined that, either the Herald from The College that recorded the Coats for Devonshire, made an error in his documentation; or that the Coat was challenged by someone in the family or by someone with a similarly recorded Coat. The entry in Burke is as follows: "Ar. on a pile gu. three crosses crosslet of the first. Crest - A cross crosslet ar." This describes a silver crest, or shield, having a triangular red pile (the symbol for an engineer or a builder) at the top, on which are found three cross crosslets, a type of cross having each of the four arms crossed. The crest above the shield is also a cross crosslet. The College concluded, after many years of research, that the Raiford Coat-of-Arms was in fact issued in 1179, but that it is similar to several Coats of other families, some of whom intermarried with Raifords over the years; namely, Chandos, Dawe, Redford and Wrayford. The College further concluded that it would be appropriate and fitting to issue and authorize a "new" Coat, a modification of the one of 1179, and to make me the propositus of the new Coat. Therefore, The College took the original Coat of the Raiford Family, the one granted in 1179, changed the background of the shield from silver to ermine, and added on the Crest a leopard's face on a silver background, since the leopard appeared on the crests of other similar and allied Coats. The "new" Raiford Coat-of-Arms was properly drawn on parchment with the appropriate colored inks, and was authenticated by having appended thereon the Coats of The College of Arms; The Duke of Norfolk, under whose aegis all Coats are granted; and that of Her Majesty, Elizabeth II. The document also has attached to it, by a ribbon and a wax seal in a gold case, the seal of The College of Arms; and the parchment is signed by Conrad Swan, Garter King of Arms. I was presented this new Coat-of-Arms in a red, oblong box with the crest of Elizabeth II embossed thereon, in a ceremony in London, on 21 May 1993, on my sixty-third birthday.

<u>The Domesday Book</u> was compiled by the Normans in 1085/6 with the object of recording all the landed property in the country, the name of the holder of the land, the number and social status of the adult population, the area of the arable land suitable for cultivation, and the amount of tax or "geld" that was being assessed on the property. In this Book, the Land of the King's Thanes lists Wereia (or Wergi) as belonging to Godwin. These two spellings devolved from the Saxon word "wearg" meaning

"felon", implying that felons may have been put to death by drowning in the nearby river, known as the Wray. Godwin, who also held many other manors, was one of the twenty-one English Thanes in Devon who was allowed to retain his estates after the Conquest, presumably because he had rendered some special service to the Conqueror. These Thanes were not a part of the King's military or civil establishment, but were employed to do services for the King away from the Royal Court, in such occupations as foresters, falcon trainers, builders (engineers), and the like.

The Manor of Wray had been carved out of the Manor of Moreton, now Moretonhampstead. During his reign from 1100 to 1135, King Henry I granted the Manor of Moreton to one of his natural sons, William de Tracy, who had a daughter, Grace, who married Sir John de Sudely. When their only son, William, became of age, he assumed his grandfather's surname, simultaneously inheriting the Manor of Moreton. On the evening of 29 December 1170, young William de Tracy, along with three other young and adventurous knights (Reginald Fitz Urse, Richard Brito and Hugh de Morville) entered Canterbury Cathedral and slew the Archbishop, Thomas à Becket, thinking that they were pleasing their King, Henry II, who had been heard to say, "Is there none who will rid me of this turbulent priest?" For their actions, the four young knights were banished by Pope Alexander III to Jerusalem, condemning them to life-long penance, never to set foot in England again. All properties of the four were taken into the King's hand once again; and from 1171, the Manors of Moreton and Wray were administered by the King's escheator for Devon. Shortly after 1174, King Henry II granted the two Manors to William de Mondeville, 3rd Earl of Essex, who subsequently granted the smaller Manor of Wray to Elias Foorde as a reward for having accompanied de Mondeville on a pilgrimage to the Holy Land in 1166. When the Earl died in 1190, the Manor of Moreton reverted to the King, Richard I (Coeur de Lion), but the Manor of Wray remained with Elias Foorde and his descendants. Since surnames were just being introduced at about this time in English history, it is plausible to assume that Elias Foorde might have been known as "Elias who lives at the ford of the Wray." In any event, when the family Coat-of-Arms was granted in 1179, it was granted in the name "Raiford."

The Manor of Wray is known today as Wray Barton Manor, the word "barton" meaning "the holding of the strong man." It is located on the eastern edge of the Dartmoor National Park, approximately one and one-half miles southeast of the village of Moretonhampstead. The Manor has been inhabited continually since 1238, as verified by the local records in Moretonhampstead. The current Manor house, built in 1615, sits on a knoll, facing the highway, with the River Wray some one hundred yards behind it. Below the current Manor house, and adjacent to it, is a "yard" completely surrounded by a stone fence bordering on the highway in front. Within this "yard", stands a wall containing a Norman arch, typical of the construction in the 12th and 13th Centuries. The remnants of another fence extend from the "yard" rearward, almost to the River Wray.

On the first day that I visited Wray Barton Manor, the air was hazy. As I stood in the "yard", the sun was setting behind me. As I looked around and tried to envisage a scene some 800 years before, when Elias Foorde lived here, here at the ford of the River Wray, I walked under the Norman arch and stopped. At that moment I heard a voice say, "You've got to be a Raiford. Welcome home." I looked up and saw a woman standing on the parapet of the current Manor house. She continued, "I've told my husband that one day a descendant of Elias Foorde would come back to the Manor. You must be he." I was overwhelmed. I spoke with the woman and her husband, who had lived there for about twenty years and who now operate Wray Barton Manor as a bed and breakfast. All in all, it was quite an experience.

📖 📖 📖

When I was serving on the Board of Management of The Cosmos Club of Washington, DC, we established reciprocity with The Arts Club in London. As a gesture of "good will", I offered to give a piano recital in The Arts Club, if that would be acceptable to them. A resounding "yes" was transmitted to the Cosmos Club and I traveled to London for my performance, on 6 October 1993. When I entered the Club on Dover Street on the afternoon of my recital, the Club Manager escorted me to the Ballroom, opened the grand piano, and presented me with a copy of A Most Agreeable Society, a history of the Arts Club written by Bernard Denvir, a member of the Club and the Vice-President of the British Section of the Internatioanl Association of Art Critics. When I inquired if it might be possible to have Mr. Denvir inscribe my copy of his book, the Club Manager said that Mr. Denvir would be in attendance that evening at my recital and would most certainly agree to my request. After my performance, several people gathered around the piano, and the Club Manager introduced me to Mr. Denvir. When I asked the octogenarian if he would honor my request to inscribe my copy of his book, he replied that he usually received five hundred pounds for his autograph. When I responded that I did not have that much currency on my person, but I would like to buy him a drink instead, he replied, "I'll take it." During our drink session, Mr. Denvir informed me of several facts about the Club, one of which was that The Arts Club had had two very famous members who had fought openly to discredit each other. The first was James McNeill Whistler, who in his youth had attended West Point but did not graduate; and the other was Oscar Wilde, who proceeded to achieve his purpose by writing <u>The Picture of Dorian Gray</u>. In later years, when I met the grandson of Oscar Wilde, he confirmed that his grandfather had written the book patterned on the life of Whistler. I was amazed that evening also to find two music lovers who could use my services.

When I first began to visit London in the pursuit of my ancestry, I was introduced to a gentleman by a West Point classmate of mine. He was a most distinguished man of letters and enjoyed a most prominent position in London Society. On our second meeting, he invited me to have lunch with him at a noted restaurant near Green Park Station. After we had been seated, and after the waiters had "kowtowed" to him as we entered the restaurant, I inquired if he had any association with the restaurant. Reluctantly, he informed me that he was the owner of one third, with a very famous British actor owning one third and a member of the Royal Family owning the last third. He further informed me that, regrettably, he would have to interrupt our luncheon for about one hour, because he had to attend the dedication of a new hospital in London. At the beginning of our main course, a waiter came over and whispered that his car had arrived. As he excused himself and left the table, I was able to see over the window curtains and saw him get into the car besides the member of the Royal Family who also owned a part interest in the restaurant. After about forty minutes, my friend returned to the table and made no comment referring to his departure or his traveling companion. We continued our discussion as before, and I was able to receive from him letters of introduction to several new friends and contacts who might be able to use my services.

On 28 April 1978, I received a letter from President Jimmy Carter thanking me for my participation in the "deliberative process" which took place regarding the transfer of the Panama Canal back to the Government of Panama. "After years of difficult negotiations and months of Senate debate, new Treaties between the United States and Panama were recently approved." I had the honor and pleasure to serve as a liaison to several individuals who became intimately involved in these discussions.

While he was in the White House, President Carter attended The First Baptist Church in Washington, DC. He also served as an Assistant Sunday School Teacher in our Adult Bible Study Class. I had previously transferred my Church membership from the First Baptist Church in Thomasville, Georgia, to the First Baptist Church in Washington. On some Sundays when he would teach our Sunday School Class, he would ask me to read the Scripture; and on the Sunday's I would teach, I would reciprocate. On one particular visit to a White House dinner, Mrs. Carter said, as Chase and I were going through the receiving line, "Tonight you won't have to read or pray, Bill. Just have a good time."

On another occasion about this same time, one of the Art Galleries on P Street in Northwest Washington had a Retrospective of Andy Warhol's works. Chase and I received an invitation to the Reception that preceded the opening. During the evening, I asked Mr. Warhol if he would sign a print of his, depicting Jimmy Carter in a block of four drawings, after I had purchased it. He agreed. The following day, I took the print to the

White House and asked The President if he would also sign it. He also agreed. In later years after checking with the Warhol cataloguer of his works, I determined that my print, signed by both the subject and the artist, is unique. It too hangs on my "I like me" wall.

📖 📖 📖

In 1980, with the Olympic Games scheduled for Moscow in the Soviet Union, I arranged for one of my AMI Board members and his son, and two additional male friends, to join with me and my three sons to attend the Games. Our schedule called for us to fly from Washington, DC, to Tokyo, Japan; from thence we would travel by ship to Nakhodka, near Vladivostok, on the eastern edge of the Soviet Union. There we were to board the Trans-Siberian Railway for an eight-day trip across eleven time zones, to arrive in Moscow for our ticketed attendance at the 1980 Games. We had been invited to stay at the U.S. Embassy while in Moscow by the then-current United States Ambassador to the Soviet Union, Mr. Thomas Watson, the former head of the IBM Corporation, who was an old friend from my former days with the Company. From Moscow, we were to fly to Paris where our wives were to meet us for a few days visit there before returning to Washington. One of the reasons that this trip was so important to me was the fact that I had been invited to write, and did so, the music for the Closing Ceremony of the Games. And then the roof fell in! The Soviet Union invaded Afghanistan, and President Carter said that America would not participate in the Games and that no American could attend. Fortunately, we were able to recoup our funds for all the tickets and the travel, but our disappointment lingered for years. A few months after the Games had ended, I received, by way of courier from the Soviet Embassy in Washington, the score of my music, with no note attached. However, at a later date, over a glass of wine at the Cosmos Club in Washington, the Cultural Attaché of the Soviet Union thanked me and expressed his personal regret that we had been unable to attend.

In the mid-1980s, Chase and I decided to attend the annual Army-Navy Football Game in Philadelphia, Pennsylvania. Rather than drive, we decided to take the train up from Washington. When we boarded at Union Station, we found that our seats on the Club Car were next to the seat of Perle Mesta, The Former United States Ambassador to the European country of Luxembourg, having been appointed by President Truman. Mrs. Mesta was affectionately known as the "Hostess with the Mostest." Having previously been introduced at The White House, our conversations were both extended and interesting, since she was quite vocal about being an Army fan. When the game was over and we had re-boarded our train, we began a discussion of the game. Our conversation was interrupted by an Air Force Lieutenant Colonel, one of the Aides-de Camp to the Chief of Staff of the Air Force, who entered the Club Car and saluted Mrs. Mesta quite formerly, saying "Madam Ambassador, I bring you greetings from The Chief of Staff of the United States Air Force, who requests that you join him in his Private Car for a Reception." Mrs. Mesta, who did not drink alcoholic beverages at all, replied, "Thank you, Colonel. Please give my best regards to the Chief of Staff and my regrets that I shall not be able to join him, as I am socializing with my friends, the Raifords." The Colonel saluted again and departed. Mrs.

Mesta then said to Chase and me, "If there is anything I despise it's a drunken flyboy."

　　　　　　　　　📖 📖 📖

On the day of the First Inauguration of President Clinton, a friend invited Chase and me to view the Inauguration Parade from the eighth floor office of his law firm, which was on Pennsylvania Avenue. He had also invited the cast of the popular television show, "Evening Shade", to be present, he having previously dated one of the cast members. Among those present were Elizabeth Ashley and Marilu Henner, along with Hal Holbrook, who previously had portrayed Mark Twain on both the stage and television. Following the Parade, our host, a former President of the Cosmos Club, invited all of us to dine together in a private dining room at the Club. Knowing of Chase's admiration for Holbrook, our host seated my wife on Holbrook's right at dinner. After a most delightful evening, Holbrook indicated that he needed to get back to his hotel because of an early flight out of DC the next morning. When he asked about getting a cab, Chase and I offered to take him back to his hotel and he accepted. It was a great thrill for Chase, and for me, to have this short but wonderfully personal time with the great Hal Holbrook.

　　　　　　　　　📖 📖 📖

During the period from 1976 until her death in 2000, Chase and I took several trips to the Caribbean. In 1976, when Rich was a Senior in High

School, we took all three boys to the U.S. owned island of St. Croix over the Easter holidays. Our accommodations were at The Buccaneer, a delightful resort on the north side of the island. As we were unpacking our luggage, the boys produced a deflated basketball which we were able to have pumped up for their games. On one particular afternoon, while standing in the lobby awaiting my turn with the concierge, I engaged a young man in a conversation about our proposed trip to Buck Island the next day. After a few preliminary questions and answers, he indicated that he was the Captain of a private yacht docked at The Buccaneer and that the owner of the yacht would not be arriving until two days hence. After he determined that our party of five was a "reasonably respectable" group, he offered to take us out to the island the next morning, to furnish sandwiches and cold drinks for everybody, and to furnish each of the five of us with the appropriate SCUBA and/or snorkeling gear. Since he was not in the business of offering these services to everyone, I was able to negotiate a very reasonable price for our trip. The desk clerk had overheard our entire discussion; and, when I looked to him for an indication of whether or not I should trust this young man, he indicated that the owners of the yacht were frequent visitors to The Buccaneer and that the Captain was a very capable pilot. We had a most delightful day on our trip to Buck Island, stopping on the way for snorkeling in our Nation's premier underwater National Park.

When our visit to St. Croix was over, we flew back to San Juan, Puerto Rico, to connect with our flight back to the States. As I checked in at the ticket counter, the agent carefully scanned my passport and noted that I had "been to some exotic world spots." I got our five boarding passes and settled in the waiting room to await our flight. In about ten minutes, my name was called on the loud speaker and I was requested to come to the desk. The agent informed me that the flight was oversold in the Tourist Section and that the airlines would like to upgrade the five of us to First Class. When we boarded the aircraft and the First Class service began, our three boys were convinced that I had "paid" the agent some "monstrous" amount just so they could have a really great vacation. It really was a great vacation.

Rich was married to Karen McCarter on 27 September 1986. They have one daughter, Rachel Alexandria, who was born on 20 September 1988. Dave married Lisa Garrett on 5 April 1986. They also have one daughter, Emily Chase, who was born on 5 October 1990. Bill married Kimberly Gheysen on 16 July 1988. To this marriage have been born three children: Michael William was born on 31 March 1992, James Andrew was born on 28 September 1994, and Nicole Ann was born on 4 September 1998.

Chase and I visited our favorite Caribbean island, Saint Martin/Sint Maarten, on several occasions. We always stayed on the Dutch side of the island but took our meals on the French side. In Grande Case, the small village on the northern side of the French sector, there is a string of superb restaurants at the water's edge. Having cocktails and watching the sun set at La Samana, on the western side of the French sector, also was a highlight of our visits. We had already made reservations for our proposed visit in January of 2001, when Chase's death occurred in October of 2000. My Doctor suggested that I should continue to make plans to go and that I should invite the three boys to go with me. This I did. Although Dave was unable to get away from his hospital duties, both Rich and Bill were able to arrange their schedules, so that Rich could come down one week and Bill the other. We had a wonderful time together, and I believe the trip was good therapy for each of us.

During Rich's visit to the island, we ate dinner one evening in one of the fine restaurants in Grande Case. The owner of the restaurant had formerly lived in Washington, DC, and had owned and operated the restaurant, La Niçoise, in Georgetown, DC. He was also an avid fan of the Washington Redskins Football Team. In fact, the walls of his restaurant on St. Martin were covered with Redskins memorabilia. Rich was so impressed with the evening and the restaurant that, upon his return to his home in California, he had a framed copy made of the sheet music of "Hail To The Redskins", which had been inscribed by the composer, Barney Breeskin, to me; and which I had previously given to Rich, since he was also an avid fan. This now hangs on the wall of the St. Martin restaurant.

📖 📖 📖

Jose Maria Figueres, a foreign graduate of the West Point Class of 1979, was elected to the Presidency of his country, Costa Rica, in 1994. The United States Delegation to his Inauguration was composed of a Member of President Clinton's Cabinet; a senior Member of the United States Senate; one of my West Point Classmates, who had been the "Plebe

Papa" or the designated mentor to Figueres during his years at West Point; and myself. During the three-day festivities, we four attended all the "official" functions, and I was able to "meet and greet" many of the other delegations to the Inaugural.

On a subsequent visit to Costa Rica, I was staying with a friend at his villa in the mountains above the capital of San José. This visit occurred only ten days after the eruption of one of Costa Rica's three active volcanoes. My friend and I decided that I should have a good view of an active volcano, so we drove as near to the top as the authorities would permit. After parking his vehicle, we then proceeded on foot up the road to the park near the crest. This is normally a popular tourist sight, but because of the recent eruption, the park was virtually closed. Not to be outdone, I walked as close to the edge as I deemed advisable. The crater was still smoking. My friend took several pictures of "the stupid tourist." The volcano remained quiet during the remainder of my visit, but erupted again two weeks hence.

📖 📖 📖

As the three boys finished their high school education, each began a career of higher learning and contributions to society. Rich received his Baccalaureate Degree from Purdue University in Aeronautical Engineering, joined the Northrop Grumman Corporation and completed his Masters Degree in Astronautical Engineering at the University of Southern California.

David completed his under-graduate work at The Massachusetts Institute of Technology (MIT) and then graduated from The Johns Hopkins University School of Medicine, where he also performed his Internship, Residency, Chief Residency and a two-year specialty fellowship in Hepatology. After ten years in Baltimore, Maryland, he moved to Tennessee to become the Chief of Liver Services, a Full Professor of Medicine and the Associate Dean for Faculty Affairs at Vanderbilt University Hospital in Nashville.

Bill attended Columbia University in New York City and played Varsity Basketball while completing his Baccalaureate Degree in Chemical Engineering, before going on to MIT for both his Masters and Doctorate Degrees in Chemical Engineering. He joined the Dupont Company after completing his formal education and has been engaged in both Manufacturing and Technology Management for the Fluoroproducts business.

📖 📖 📖

In the early-1990s, one of my fellow West Point graduates and his wife, both of whom were dear friends of both Chase and me, decided to give up their lovely home in Washington and retire to an assisted living facility near the home of their daughter and son-in-law in Connecticut. The husband had retired from the military with the rank of Colonel, and then served with the OSS and its successor, the CIA, and had two most distinguished military and civilian records of accomplishments. Chase and I gave a dinner party at our home in Maryland and invited them and also a couple who were mutual friends of both ours and the Colonel and his wife. Associate Justice of the United States Supreme Court Sandra Day O'Connor and her husband, John, always added an aura of distinction to any party. When we had finished dinner and had retired to the living room for coffee and liqueurs, John O'Connor kicked off his shoes. Sandra exclaimed, "John, what are you doing"? "Making myself at home", was his reply. "Chase, do you mind?"

At another dinner party in Washington in 1997, The Justice asked me how things were going with West Point's Bicentennial. I told her that everything was going very well, but that I had one problem. We were preparing to create a Women's Affairs Committee for the Bicentennial, so that we could have input and opinions on each of the events being planned, from a woman's point of view. I opined that the female graduates of the Academy, which first occurred in 1980, had not attained sufficient rank for me to appoint one to the Chairmanship. (The Chairmen of the Committees were either Colonels, one-, two-, three-, or four-star Generals, Ambassadors, or civilians of equal rank.) I asked her if she had any suggestions as to who I might consider for the post. She replied, "Let me do it. I would be pleased to work on West Point's Bicentennial." When I apologized for having put her on the spot, she said, "Nonsense. I would be honored to be on your Committee." She assumed the Chairmanship of the Women's Affairs Committee and attended our next annual meeting of all Committees and Staff, held in the Conference Room of The Secretary of Defense in the Pentagon on the second Monday in September. During her tenure, until the Bicentennial events began in late 2001, she was an active and most helpful participant.

In the Spring of 2002, I suggested to the Secretary of the Army that I would like to commend each of the eighty-five Bicentennial Committee members and staff; and in my opinion, a "certificate of thanks" would not suffice. Since the Secretary has an option of awarding one of three medals for "outstanding service" to the Army, I presented him with three lists of those potential awardees who had served on the Committees: for up to two years, from two to five years, and for service over five years. I further suggested that all Committee Chairmen receive the highest of the three awards. The Secretary of the Army approved my suggestions "in toto"; and in the Fall of 2002, at a ceremony in Cullum Hall at West Point, I had the honor of decorating each of my Committee Chairmen and Staff with the highest award, and then each Committee Chairman decorated the members of his Committee with one of the two other awards. Justice O'Connor was unable to attend that ceremony, but subsequently, in her Chambers in The Supreme Court Building in Washington, the award was presented. She told me how pleased she was to have been decorated for her services.

At a "black tie" dinner of the Chevaliers du Tastevin in Washington, which was held in the dining room of The Supreme Court of the United States, because the "Host" that evening was The Chief Justice, Warren E. Burger; my middle son, Dave, was in town on business, and I had inquired if it might be possible to bring him "as my dinner partner" since Chase was unable to attend due to her illness. It was during the cocktail hour that the photographer took a picture of Dave and me standing with the Chief Justice. When the picture was delivered to me a few days later, I telephoned his Secretary and asked if the Chief Justice would autograph the picture to my son. Receiving a positive response, I hand delivered it to the Court. Several days later, the autographed picture came in the mail and the envelope was address to "General William R. Raiford." I telephoned the Secretary and explained that, although I was a West Point graduate, I had never risen to the rank of General, and I wanted to correct any false impression the Chief Justice may have had. The Secretary asked me to hold. The Chief Justice came on the line and said, "Bill, I appreciate your call and I knew that you were not a retired General, but you should have been."

In 1981, Chase was diagnosed with Crohn's disease, an insidious disease that attacks the intestines. There is no known cause or cure. Periodic surgeries to remove the infected portions of the bowel are a requirement. The daily ingestion of Prednisone for over seventeen years kept the disease at bay. However, after many years of "living with it", her condition began to deteriorate in 1999. She developed a heart murmur and began to lose considerable weight. But, with an indomitable spirit, she kept going.

When she had her first surgery, it occurred just one week before she and I were to have attended a fund-raising dinner for the Smith Club of Washington, DC. George Will, the noted author and syndicated columnist, was to be the speaker. When I telephoned George, an old friend of ours, and told him that we would not be able to attend due to Chase's hospitalization, he asked in which hospital she was confined. That evening, as I was sitting by her bedside, her telephone rang. She answered with a very weak voice, "Hello." A pause. "Who?" Another pause. "The hell you say." Another pause. "Thank you, George. I really appreciate your call", she said. We both did.

⸻

In 1996, for our fortieth wedding anniversary, Chase and I traveled overnight via train through the gorges of West Virginia to Chicago. After a lunch in The Pump Room and an afternoon of shopping at Marshall Field's Department Store, we boarded the AMTRAK liner, "The Pioneer", and proceeded cross-country to Kansas City, Denver, and Salt Lake City, then on to Portland and Seattle. After a few days in Seattle, we boarded a ferry to Vancouver Island and stayed two nights at The Princess, where we enjoyed tea and scones with Devonshire cream at 4 o'clock each afternoon. A visit to Bouchart Gardens was thrilling. Then we took another ferry to Vancouver and boarded the Canadian National for a rail trip eastward across Canada, stopping at Jasper National Park, renting a car, and driving southward through the Columbia Ice Fields to Lake Louise for a two day visit. Returning to Jasper, we again boarded the train and continued our journey to Toronto, Niagara Falls and back to Washington. We both had loved trains since childhood and this was the trip that we both needed at that time.

⸻

In the fall of 2000, Bill was scheduled for a laminectomy, which would require that he be bedridden for approximately eight weeks. Bill requested that his mother come to Fayetteville, North Carolina, to assist his wife, Kim, and their three children, with the situation to be caused by his surgery. Chase and I talked about whether or not she should go. She really did not feel up to the task, but felt that she was needed, and she wanted to be of any assistance that she could. So I took her to the train in Washington and Bill and Kim met her in Fayetteville some eight hours later, on a Thursday evening. Bill's surgery was on Friday and he came home over the weekend, confined to his bed for the expected eight weeks. I telephoned Chase each evening. On each occasion she replied that, although she was tired, she felt that she was needed and was glad to be there. I was scheduled to fly from Dulles International outside Washington to Paris on Monday evening for business pertaining to the Society of the Cincinnati, of which I was then the President General. I spoke with her just before boarding the plane, receiving assurance from her that I should go and that she would be all right. I landed in Paris on Tuesday morning, checked into my hotel and made the contacts that were scheduled. While meeting with personnel from our American Embassy, I sensed that all was not well and excused myself to go back to my hotel room. As I entered the room, the telephone rang. It was my son, Rich, calling to tell me that his mother was dead. She had gotten up from the dinner table, gone into the bathroom off the kitchen, locked the door, and fallen to the floor. Death was instantaneous. I could not get a flight from Paris back to the States until noon the next day. In the interim, Dave flew from Nashville to Fayetteville and took care of all the arrangements required for the disposition of Chase's body. Rich flew from Los Angeles to Dulles International and met me when I arrived from Paris. He and I made all the funeral arrangements locally while Dave arranged for Chase's body to arrive by train from Fayetteville. A few days later, we had a viewing at a Funeral Home in Bethesda, Maryland. A friend arranged for Bill to come up from Fayetteville in a van converted with a mattress, for the viewing, after which Chase's body was cremated. An urn was sent down from West Point and her ashes were placed therein, but the inurnment in the Columbarium under the Old Cadet Chapel at The United States Military Academy was delayed for about six weeks until Bill was able to travel.

On the day I arrived back in Old Farm from Paris, two days after Chase's death on 18 October, I noticed that one of the white azalea bushes at the corner of our patio had one single white flower. I took a photograph of this single white bloom, which lasted until the day of the viewing at the funeral home.

After Chase's death, many friends and relatives brought food and flowers to our home, and the cards and letters began to arrive, telling me how much Chase had meant to each of the writers. I began to build a file, so that my three boys could read all of them when next they came home. The file continued to grow almost daily for over a year. Finally I began a scrap book of the cards and letters, displaying each so that they could be easily read. When the first book was completely filled, I began a second. The last letter arrived almost three years after Chase's death. The entire collection of expressions of condolence has exceeded five hundred items.

In March of 2001, I retired from Salomon Smith Barney, the last of the investment firms with which I had been associated since bringing my company, AMI, to E.F. Hutton in 1985. I came to Thomasville in April to conclude some business and to look around for a possible place to retire. As I drove by the house on Warren Avenue where we had lived during the years 1934-36, the sign in the yard caught my attention: "Historic Home For Sale." I drove to the offices of Thomasville Landmarks and negotiated a down payment for the purchase. After some further discussions, I contracted to purchase 318 Warren Avenue in " a completed condition." When the renovation of this 1884 house was finally finished, I signed for the property on 17 October and the movers delivered my belongings on 18 October, one year to the day after Chase's death.

Immediately after Chase's death, I began to grow a full beard again. I had had one in the early 1980s when I first began traveling to the Middle East. This time it was a manifestation of my grief. In the Fall of 2003, I awoke one morning at about 0230 and perceived that I had received a message from the Lord which said two things: (1) Your grief is over; shed your old skin; and (2) You are going on a trip and I shall be with you. I immediately went to the bathroom and shaved off my beard. In the morning service at the First Baptist Church the following Sunday, my Preacher, The Reverend Dr. Dan Spencer, indicated that the Church would be sending a group of volunteers to Thailand as Missionaries. I joined the group of volunteers and was accepted for the January, 2004, trip, but I really did not know why I was going or what my purpose on the trip would be. When we arrived in Bangkok, we traveled by bus to the small coastal town of Pattaya, the popular docking point for the Chinese visitors coming from the mainland on holiday. On one particular morning, I was given several Bibles, printed in both Mandarin and English, and was told to sit in the lobby of a certain hotel and read and pray. If anyone asked me for a Bible, I was to give it to them, but I was not to solicit anyone to receive it. So I began to read and pray. This lasted for about ninety minutes. No takers. I finally said to the

Lord in prayer, "Either Your line is busy, or I am not getting through to You. I must be in the wrong place. I'm going to move. Amen." Upon opening my eyes, I noted that a Chinese gentleman had settled into the chair next to mine. In my best Mandarin Chinese, I greeted him: "Nee-how." He responded, "Good morning, sir, and how are you?" Startled, I replied, "Fine, thank you, and your English is beautiful." He replied, "I live in Albany, Georgia", (only 60 miles from Thomasville. He even pronounced it correctly: All-benny!) After an extended conversation in which I discovered that both he and his wife, her sister and her sister's husband were all Christians and had been for about thirty years; he said, "You will never know how important your work here is. You will give a few Bibles to a few Chinese who will take them back to the mainland and will read them, alone or with friends, possibly hundreds will get to read each Bible. You will never know how many you may have led to Christ." My cup runneth over! Right then, I knelt and thanked the Lord for sending me on that trip and giving me another opportunity to witness for Him.

In 1966, I was elected to membership in Mensa; and in 1971, I was inducted into Intertel. In 1975, I was elected to Who's Who in the East. In 1988, the Nobel Peace Prize was awarded to the United Nations Peace-keeping Forces. As a member of the United Nations Peace-keeping Forces serving in the Korean War, I was informed that I was entitled to receive this award. I received a scroll certifying that "1 Lt. William R. Raiford served as a member of the United Nations Peace-keeping Forces, prior to the Norwegian Nobel Committee's awarding of the Nobel Peace Prize to the United Nations Peace-keeping Forces, on the 10th Day of

December 1988." The scroll is signed "Jergen Kosmond, Minister of Defence, Norway." I have had the medal framed, along with the scroll, for my "I like me" room, and I wear the miniature of the medal with my other decorations on my formal attire.

In 1993, I was appointed Investment Advisor for the Harry S. Truman Scholarship Foundation, the sole Financial Advisor to this Federal Agency.

In 1996, I was decorated by the President of the French Republic, Jacques Chirac, with L'Ordre National du Mérite with the rank of Officer. In 2001, I was again decorated by the President of the French Republic, this time with L'Ordre National de La Légion d'Honneur with the rank of Officer. Also in 2001, I was named Chairman of l'Institut de la Maison de Bourbon des Etats-Unis by the Board of the Institute in France. This Organization is charged with building better relations between The United States and France through lectures, newspaper editorials and exchange visits. One of the important events in the history of our Country, which most Americans appear to have forgotten, or never knew, is the fact that, had it not been for the French at Yorktown, Virginia, in 1781, we would not be a country today. King Louis XVI sent to General Washington three billion gold livres (pounds), a fleet of ships and approximately 6,000 troops, all with the intent of defeating the British. There are about 2,400 French bodies buried on American soil as a result of that conflict. Each time that I have an opportunity to speak on this subject in France, I point out these facts and thank the French once again for their help in securing our freedom. I also hasten to point out that, had it not been for the Americans in World Wars I and II, neither would France be a country today speaking French in stead of

German. As General De Gaulle told President Eisenhower, "We saved each other."

In 1961, I was inducted into membership in the Society of the Cincinnati, the oldest patriotic Society in the United States, having been founded by the Officers of the Continental Army on 13 May 1783 at the Headquarters of Baron von Steuben, in the Verplanck House in Fishkill, New York. Membership in the Society is restricted to male descendants of Regular Officers who served in the American War for Independence for at least three years; or who had been in service at the conclusion of the War, at Yorktown in 1781; or who had been killed in service. My ancestor, known as my propositus, was Maurice Raiford, who served in the Fourth North Carolina Continental Regiment, in excess of three years.

In the Institution of the Society, its founders explained their choice of its name, thusly: "The Officers of the American Army, having been taken from the citizens of America, possess high veneration for the character of that illustrious Roman, Lucius Quintius Cincinnatus, and being resolved to follow his example, by returning to their citizenship, they think they may, with propriety, denominate themselves the Society of the Cincinnati." According to Livy in his History of Rome; in the 5th Century B.C., Cincinnatus was summoned to Rome and appointed Dictator for six months, and was bade to "come forthwith to the defense of the land." Under his lead the invading hoards were driven out.

Thereupon, he resigned the Dictatorship and returned to the plow. This he did - - twice.

According to the Institution of the Society, "The following principles shall be immutable and form the basis of the Society of the Cincinnati:

"An incessant attention to preserve inviolate those exalted rights and liberties of human nature, for which they have fought and died, and without which the high rank of a rational being is a curse instead of a blessing.

"An unalterable determination to promote and cherish, between the respective States, that union and national honor so essentially necessary to their happiness, and the future dignity of the American empire.

"To render permanent the cordial affection subsisting among the officers. This spirit will dictate brotherly kindness in all things, and particularly extend to the most substantial acts of beneficence, according to the ability of the Society, towards those officers and their families, who unfortunately may be under the necessity of receiving it."

During my years in this Society, I have served as Marshall and on the Standing Committee of the North Carolina Society; and as Secretary of the Corporation, and on the Board of Directors of the General Society. In addition, I was a co-founder of the Society's French and American Scholars Committee in 1964 and served thereon until 1992, serving the last six years as the Committee Chairman. This Committee selects young men who are sons of members, or members in their own right, to visit in France and America, at no expense to them, for a period of four-to-five weeks, to become better acquainted with the country and its people.

At a dinner party in Washington at the home of a member of the Staff of the Embassy of France, twelve guests were seated at a magnificently decorated table in such a manner that on the right and left of each person sat someone who spoke not only his or her first language but another language as well. Chase had the honor to be seated on the right of the host. As the dessert was brought to the table and placed in front of the hostess, who was seated at the opposite end from her husband, she picked up a serving utensil to attack delicately the beautifully prepared macaroon tree which had been placed before her. Due to over-caramelizing, the top of the tree refused to budge. She tapped it harder. No success. As she arose from her seat and gave the top of the tree a forceful whack, the top piece of the tree broke off and traveled the entire length of the table and lodged in the top of Chase's gown. Without batting an eye, and in a typically Gallic manner, the host, a dear friend of both Chase's and mine, picked up his dessert spoon, wiped it on his napkin and said to Chase, "May I be of any assistance"? The laughter at an already relaxed dinner was delightful.

Later in the dinner, while everyone was chatting before retiring to the drawing room for coffee and liqueurs, the host announced that we would play a game called "Gossip." One person begins by saying something in his first language which is in common with the person on his or her right, who then must translate that comment into the other language spoken in common with the person on his or her right, and so on around the table. Truly a United Nations potential mix -up. Our host whispered in Chase's ear the name of the Rimsky-Korsakov opera, "Le Coq d'Or." She in turn said to the gentleman on her right, "The Golden Rooster." By the time the phrase had gotten to the wife of the Greek Ambassador, she announced in perfect English, "I can't say that in polite Society." When the laughter had subsided, I related a similar experience when I was with IBM in Kingston, New York. We were working on the first translation machine to have been designed and built using a digital computer. One of the Engineers working with our group was Chinese, so he chose to input into the machine the English phrase "Out of sight; out of mind." When the printer displayed the Chinese characters into which the machine had translated, The Chinese Engineer then re-entered into the machine the same characters, which came back to him as "Invisible; insane."

In 1981, my son, David Shepherd Raiford, became a member of the North Carolina Society of the Cincinnati, representing his great-great-great-grand uncle, Captain and Brevet Major Robert Raiford, Second Regiment, North Carolina Continental Line.

In 1983, my son, William Postell Raiford, became a member of the North Carolina Society of the Cincinnati, representing his great-great-great-grandfather, Captain John Hodges, Fifth Regiment, North Carolina Continental Line.

And in 2003, I resigned my membership in the Society so that my eldest son, Richard Renz Raiford, could become a member of the North

Carolina Society of the Cincinnati, representing his great-great-great-grandfather, Lieutenant Maurice Raiford, Fourth Regiment, North Carolina Continental Line.

Subsequent to my resignation therefrom, The North Carolina Society of the Cincinnati invested me as an Honorary Member.

At the Triennial of the Society, held in France in 1974, one of the events was the unveiling of a bronze statue of His Excellency, the Count de Rochambeau, Commander in Chief of the French Army during the American Revolution, in his home town of Vendôme. The original statue had been taken down by the Germans during World War II to be melted for their war effort. Several of us Society members had engaged a team to search for the original mold which was finally located in the attic of the Museum of the Beaux Arts in Paris. A new statue was cast and was erected on the site of the original. The statue was presented as a gift from the General Society but had, in fact, been paid for by contributions solicited by The President General from only twelve members, the majority of whom were members of the Society of our President General, North Carolina. Attending the ceremony was the President General of the Society of the Cincinnati and the other five General Officers; the United States Ambassador to the Republic of France; the French Ambassador to the United States; the Mayor of the City of Vendôme, the Delegates and Alternate Delegates of the Society to the Triennial; and their wives; and the townspeople of Vendôme. The entire City had closed for the day. After the ceremonies, everyone was invited for a champagne buffet in the local Sports Recreation Hall, which had been decorated in red, white and blue, with both French and American flags in profusion. The townspeople were openly joyous and grateful for the efforts of the Americans, in restoring their "native son" to his place of honor in their City square.

One of my more humorous memories of the Cincinnati occurred in the Spring of 1976 when my oldest son, Rich, was a Senior in High School. Chase and I were scheduled to attend the formal Spring Dinner at The Anderson House in Washington, DC, when about two in the afternoon of the day of the Dinner, Chase was not feeling well and was unable to attend. I invited Rich to accompany me in his mother's place. "But I don't have a tux," he said. "Not to worry", said I. "We'll just go up on the Pike (Rockville Pike) and rent you one." This we did. As we were getting dressed that evening, Chase instructed Rich to remember his table manners and to "follow the others at the table." Everything was going along "swimmingly"; Rich was using the right utensil with each of the five courses of the dinner. And then came the finger bowls. Rich looked around the table, and not waiting for anyone else, he promptly and correctly placed the doily and the bowl in the proper place in front of him, and put the dessert fork and spoon on the correct sides of his plate. As I was seated across the table directly in front of him, I caught his eye as he gave me a grin and a wink. All I could think of was the expression my mother had often said: "It took; it took", meaning that her instructions had not been wasted on deaf ears.

In 1976, during the Bicentennial of the United States, the Society of the Cincinnati inducted, as an Honorary Member for life, the President of the Republic of France, His Excellency Valéry Giscard d'Estaing. Similarly, in 1983, during the Bicentennial of The Society of the Cincinnati, the Society inducted, as an Honorary Member for life, The President of the United States, His Excellency Ronald Wilson Reagan. During both ceremonies, as one of the younger members of the Board of Directors of the Society, I had the honor of holding the flag of the Country of the Honoree.

In 1995, at the Triennial Convocation of the Society in Boston, Massachusetts, on the 19th day of May, the evening of the day of my mother's death, I was elected to the position of Vice President General. I served in that capacity for three years. Then in 1998, at the Triennial Convocation held in Charleston, South Carolina, I was elected the thirty-second President General of the Society. (General George Washington had been the first President General.) During my term of office, the renovation of our Society's Headquarters in Washington, DC, the Anderson House, was completed; and the 200th Anniversary of the death of General Washington was commemorated at Mount Vernon, the home of the first President of the United States. On that occasion, after the completion of the ceremonies at The Mansion; and wearing the Diamond Eagle, the badge of office designed by Major Pierre l'Enfant and made by the Court Jeweler to King Louis XVI, and presented to General Washington in Philadelphia, Pennsylvania, in 1784, by the Officers and Men of the French Navy, and having been worn by every successive President General; I led the procession down the hill from The Mansion to the crypt containing the remains of the General and his wife, Martha. The iron gates were opened and I stepped into the crypt alone.

Placing my hand on the sarcophagus of the General, I felt an electric shock throughout my body. What an honor to represent the General and to wear his Eagle. It was a most humbling experience.

On 30 June 1997, I had the pleasure of visiting La Grange, the ancestral home of the Marquis de Lafayette, a few miles east of Paris, France. I was given a personal tour of the home by Comte René de Chambrun, the ninety-six year old g-g-g-grandson of the Marquis himself. Upon my departure, the Comte presented me with an 1824 engraving of his ancestor and inscribed it in the border: "For Bill from René de Chambrun."

In 1998, The Society of the Cincinnati engaged three Professors of History at West Point, Kenneth E. Hamburger, Joseph R. Fischer and Steven C. Gravlin, to create a text on the American Revolution that would be suitable for fifth graders. The result of their efforts, entitled <u>Why America is Free - A History of the Founding of the American Republic 1750-1800</u>, was published by the Society in conjunction with The Ladies of Mount Vernon, the owners of the home of our First President, General George Washington. The text follows a fictitious boy and his family during this fifty-year period and allows the reader to be intimately involved in the creation of the Republic. The cost of the publication of 10,000 copies was borne by the Society. The first printing was distributed, at no cost, to the intermediate schools throughout "the thirteen original colonies." It is also sold in the gift shop at Mount Vernon. Expanding its reach to additional States, a second printing, and a third were required. Now in its fourth printing, this volume has been seen and possibly read by over five million students throughout the United States. I have the honor to have been asked to be one of the editors of the text.

In May of 2001, when my term of office as President General was ending, the Triennial Convocation was held in Paris. What an eventful four days that was! The three highlights of that visit to France included, first, the March of all attendees up the Champ Elysées, stopping all vehicular traffic around the Arc de Triomphe during the rush hour, while the band was playing, the flags flying, and several of us, representing the United States, France, the Society of the Cincinnati and the Institut de la Legion d'Honneur lay wreaths at the Tomb of the Unknowns, and all five hundred of us sang the National Anthems of our two countries. The second highlight was my receipt of the Legion of Honor in the Hôtel de Salm, the Headquarters of the Legion d'Honneur. And the third, was the Saturday evening dinner held in the Hall of Battles in The Palace of Versailles. As the Master of Ceremonies at that dinner, I had the honor and the privilege to introduce the dignitaries present, the chief one of whom was His Royal Highness, Louis, Prince de Bourbon, duc d'Anjou, a member of the Society of the Cincinnati of France, representing his ancestor, King Louis XVI. Prince Louis is the Pretender to the thrones of both France and Spain, being directly descended from King Louis XIV of France and King Alphonse XIII of Spain. In May of 2002, Prince Louis visited Thomasville as my house guest on Warren Avenue and, as a gesture of good will between our two countries, planted an oak tree in the vacant lot on the corner of Warren Avenue and Love Street. The Mayor of Thomasville and Members of the City Council were present for that event.

In November of 2004, I had the pleasure of attending the wedding of Prince Louis in the Dominican Republic. He was married to Maria Margarita Vargas from Caracas, Venezuela. The ceremony was conducted under a canopy in front of the Church where five hundred guests were seated among faux marble columns entwined with real white orchids.

At the ceremony, the National Orchestra of Caracas and the National Chorus of Venezuela rendered Handel's "Hallelujah" Chorus. Buses then ferried the guests to the estate of the bride's parents for a sit-down dinner under tents for 1,700 guests.

On the 8th of June 2004, in the Basilica of St. Denis in Paris, the heart of the young King Louis XVII was formally buried in the crypt near his parents, King Louis XVI and his Queen, Marie Antoinette. After his parents were beheaded in the Place de la Concorde in Paris, the ten-year old child was taken to the Temple, a prison in the Third Arrondissement, or District, of the City, where he was kept, deprived, and abused for two years until his death. The Doctor who performed the official autopsy, removed the child's heart and placed it in a crystal urn. For over two hundred years, it was carefully guarded and passed among many members of the Royal Families of Europe. In 1995, two separate DNA tests were made, one in Belgium and one in Germany; where it was proved that the relic was the heart of King Louis XVII. The Ceremony, officially designated as "Déposition solennelle du coeur de Louis XVII dans la chapelle des Bourbons de la crypte de la cathédrale basilique de Saint-Denis", was attended by a host of dignitaries and the general public. The Comité d'honneur, or Committee of Honor, was led by Monseigneur Louis de Bourbon, duc d'Anjou, The Pretender to the Throne of France and the last in over one thousand years of the Bourbon line. He was followed by The Archduke Otto de Habsbourg Lorraine, the Duc de Parme, the Queen of Roumania, the Ambassador of Austria, the Ambassador of Switzerland, Prince Nicolas Romanov, the Prince of Savoy, and other members of Royalty from the Houses throughout Europe. Next in line were the current General Officers of the Society of the Cincinnati. I had the honor, as a Past President General of the Society, to occupy position number forty-six on the list of eighty-seven. After the ceremonies in the Basilica, Prince Louis stepped forward and retrieved the crystal urn from the altar where it had reposed during the ceremonies. As he began the procession down the steps to the crypt, each of us on the Committee of Honor followed in succession and gathered around the graves of King Louis XVI and his Queen, Marie Antoinette, for the final burial rites. After the ceremonies, a seated luncheon was held in the Gardens of the Basilica. Prince Louis asked me to accompany him and make the introductions at each of the more than thirty tables, each seating eight guests. It was truly a great honor for me and a most memorable experience.

In 2004, I had an opportunity to "touch base" once again at several stops in the world. I flew from Atlanta, Georgia, to Tokyo, Japan; then on to Bangkok, Thailand. From there I flew to Colombo, Sri Lanka, where I had a meeting with Sir Arthur C. Clarke who inscribed my first edition copy of his classic book, <u>2001: A Space Odyssey</u>. Then it was on to the Emirates in the Persian Gulf. This time, my stop was in Dubai. The Emirates have changed significantly since my first visit there in 1981. The skyscrapers and the neon signs in English indicated that change has taken place rather dramatically. From Dubai, it was on to Paris and then back to Atlanta. In all of my travels over the past thirty-plus years, this was the first time I had circumnavigated the globe in one continuous trip. While I am no longer an Advisor to the DIA, it has been an honor and a privilege to have served my Country for over fifty years. In 2003, I received from the West Point Society of the District of Columbia "The Castle Award", a silver tray awarded "To William R. Raiford For Outstanding Service and Dedication to his Country and Alma Mater." This award was named for Colonel Benjamin Frederick Castle, West Point Class of 1907, a founding member of that Society and with whom I had the pleasure of serving on the Board of Directors.

In 2005, I decided to make one "final" trip, to re-visit many old friends and contacts, and to say "hello" to a few people I only knew by name, having never met in person. I drove from Thomasville to Atlanta and parked my car on Post at Fort McPherson, having previously received permission to do so. I flew from Atlanta to Paris, France, and then on to Rome, Italy. After a few days in Rome, I boarded a train and traveled northward to Padova (Padua), where I spent three days. During my visit to Padova, I viewed the frescoes of Giotto, which I had wanted to see for many years, since I had long ago been given a framed, illuminated page by my mother-in-law. Mary had acquired this page at a flea market in Firenze (Florence) on her honeymoon there in 1929. She paid the equivalence of fifty cents. I had taken the page to the Curator at The National Gallery of Art in Washington, DC, who assisted me in having it cleaned, stretched, and properly conserved after it had hung in Mary's garage for so many years. It was then taken to the Walters Art Gallery in Baltimore, Maryland, for authentication and an opinion. After about six months of study and analysis, the page was returned to me with a written analysis, translation and authentication. The translation of the Latin text is as follows: "In Thee is my spirit refreshed which was consecrated to the Lord from birth." The page is identified as an "Antiphon for a Saint's Day (St. Jerome). Northern Italian – 14th Century. Attributed to the School of Giotto (1260-1336)". In the initial "I" of the text at the top left of the page, there is a square colored painting of The Christ and his Disciples around a table, "The Last Supper." A floral design of pink and blue flowers, green leaves and gold dots appears on the left of the text and across the bottom of the page. In the bottom center, among the floral design, is a circular painting of St. Jerome. The page itself has been authenticated with absolute certainty. However, the paintings at the top and bottom are identified only as "the School of Giotto." I had hoped that "the School of" could be omitted, but the experts have said that, while some of the brush strokes are similar to those of Giotto himself, there are enough different unidentifiable strokes to suggest that others within his workshop probably assisted the master in this endeavor. It is still a great work of art and I am pleased to have it in my collection. After its authentication, it was then framed with the assistance of the personnel at The National Gallery of Art in Washington, DC. It now hangs in my living room in a special place of honor.

Returning to Rome by train for a few more days in the capital city, I attended an outdoor performance at the Baths of Caracalla of Giuseppe Verdi's "Aida." Through the intercession of a friend, I was taken backstage after the performance to meet the principals, who invited me to join them for dinner at the home of my friend's lady friend. The entire group of musicians sat down to dinner at 2 AM, and at about 3:30, I was invited to take the bass part in the "The Sextet" ("Chi mi frena") from Act II, Scene 2, of Gaetano Donizetti's opera "Lucia de Lammermoor." I slept in, later that morning! The next morning, I took the train to Napoli (Naples) where I had engaged a car and driver for the trip down the coast, stopping at Pompeii en route to the Amalfi Coast. I stayed one week in Positano during which I visited some of the great tourist attractions in the vicinity. On a Sunday morning, I took a boat over to the island of Capri and, rejecting the funicula (tramway), I climbed the 2,200 steps to the top of the island and the center of the town. There is a tradition on Capri that, if you sit in the center of the town for one hour, you will meet someone that you know. After doing so for about ninety minutes, I started to leave, when a young couple sat down beside me. "Are you by any chance Americans?", I asked. "No, we're British", came the response. Not to be discouraged, I continued. "My family came to America from Devon in the 17th Century. They had lived near Moretonhampstead." "Oh," came the second response. "We live in Moretonhampstead." I continued. "My family's home is called Wray Barton Manor." "We know it well and have visited it often. Its 12th Century, you know." While I really did not find anyone I knew in Capri, I considered this exchange to be close enough for Government work!

After a most pleasant week on the Amalfi Coast, my car and driver headed northward for Naples, stopping en route at Erculani, or as we Americans know it, Herculaneum. I found this ancient site to be much more interesting than Pompeii – cleaner in its excavations and not so "touristy." After a few days in Naples, I boarded another train and returned to Rome, where another car and driver took me to the seaport of Rome, Civittavecchia, where I boarded a ship for an eleven-day cruise of the Greek Isles and Asia Minor. I visited Mykonos, Santorini (allegedly the site of the civilization Atlantis) and Rhodes in the Aegean Sea before sailing into the port near Ephesus. My driver took me to the place where Paul had written several of his Epistles and had preached in the marvelous amphitheatre which seated about twenty-five thousand. My next stop was Istanbul. The Blue Mosque is a wonderful attraction, as is the Palace of the Emperors. However, the vehicular traffic in Istanbul is frightful. Almost no one obeys the traffic signals, and run-ins and fender benders are daily occurrences. Shopping at the Bazaar can be daunting, for there are over 3,500 individual shops under one roof! As one passes over the bridge linking Europe with Asia, the view is quite impressive.

Returning to my ship, I spent a pleasant day and night en route to the port of Piraeus, Greece. An Officer friend in the Greek Air Force met me at the dock and took me to visit the Acropolis in the heart of Athens. When it came time to have lunch, we drove to the apartment of another friend, on the northern outskirts of the city. We then drove to a very popular restaurant and had a marvelous Greek lunch served family style. We were all having such a wonderful time together, talking about our past associations, that I completely forgot that my ship was sailing from Piraeus at 1700 hours. When I looked at my watch, it was then 1630 and we were thirty-five miles from the port. "Not to worry", said my Air Force friend. "We'll just go get your passport from the Port Authority and you can stay with me tonight." This we did. And, of course, we had to have another great Greek meal. The next morning, the parents of my host arrived and prepared a breakfast of yogurt and pastries to accompany the Greek coffee. Then they took me to the Athens Airport where I boarded my plane for Naples, where I would re-board my ship the following day for the remainder of the trip back to Rome. The only flight I could get to Naples from Athens was by way of Frankfurt, Germany, which allowed me to have lunch with another friend. When I arrived in Naples late in the afternoon, I took a cab to the Hotel Mediterraneo, a member of the Marriott Hotel chain. As I entered the lobby, tired and dirty, without luggage, I explained my predicament to the concierge, who patiently listened to my plight. In my explanation, I added that I had lived in Washington, DC, for many years, and that I knew the Marriott Family well. When I asked if there might be a room for me for the night until I could board my ship the next morning, I was graciously accommodated with a beautiful suite! After I had showered, put on the same clothes and returned to the lobby for the evening meal, I was escorted by the concierge to the rooftop restaurant, where I enjoyed a magnificent meal as I viewed Mount Vesuvius to the northeast, the Bay of Naples and Sorrento to the south and the Isle of Capri to the southwest.

The next morning, I re-boarded my ship and was welcomed most effusively by the ship's personnel, some of whom had been convinced that I had fallen overboard in the Aegean Sea! The next morning, we docked back at Civittavecchia and I transferred to the Hilton Hotel near the Rome Airport for an overnight. I then flew from Rome back to Paris, where I boarded a TGV (Train Grande Vitesse – high speed train) bound for the city of Libourne, near Bordeaux. There I was met by an old friend whom I had known for about twenty years, who drove me to his château in the Côtes de Castillon. I spent a week with him and his family and then was picked up by another friend and his wife and driven to their home in the Dordogne for another week's visit. Returning to Paris, I flew from the Charles de Gaulle Airport back to Atlanta, picked up my car at Fort McPherson and returned to Thomasville after a most pleasant and wonderful sixty-five day excursion.

📖 📖 📖

In 2005, I was elected to the Board of Directors of Thomasville Landmarks, Incorporated, for a three-year term. This in an organization created and dedicated to the restoration and preservation of historical landmarks in Thomasville and Thomas County, Georgia. One of its achievements is the listing of the Love Street-Warren Avenue Historical

District on the National Register. My home is situated within this District.

Another reason that I love Thomasville and Thomas County is all the plantations. Between Thomasville and Tallahassee, Florida, there are seventy-one plantations, comprising over 330,000 acres, most in pristine condition and most devoted to the preservation of that condition. There are many hunting preserves, and the residents and friends look forward each year to the hunting seasons, which draw many enthusiasts for deer, quail and wild turkey. The road between these two major cities has been officially designated as "Plantation Parkway."

Prior to the compiling of this work, I have published two books; namely, <u>West Point and The Society of the Cincinnati</u>, in 1967, which covers a brief exposition of each of the West Pointers who later became members of the Society; and <u>The History of the Raiford Family</u> in 1989, which covers eight hundred years of family history since the granting of the Coat-of-Arms in 1179 in England during the reign of King Henry II. However, I have never published any of my musical compositions nor have I ever charged for any concert or recital that I have presented. Its just not my "thing."

Over the years, I have been fortunate to have been able to collect books and other memorabilia written by friends and associates and to have those items inscribed for my personal library. In my collection are items from every American President from Truman through Reagan, other Heads of State, Ambassadors, Diplomats, Military Men and Women, U.S. Supreme Court Justices, Musicians, Artists, Poets, Nobel Laureates and just plain, ordinary people like myself. I have over six hundred books and other inscribed items in my collection. Some of my more prized items include the autographs and inscriptions of President Truman's Secretary of State Dean Acheson and Mrs. (Alice) Acheson; "Buzz" Aldrin; Steve Allen; Stephen Ambrose; Mikhail Baryshnikov; Herblock; Chief Justice Warren E. Burger; Joe Califano; President Jimmy Carter and his wife, Rosalynn Carter; two Presidents of the Republic of France, Valéry Giscard d'Estaing and Jacques Chirac; Tom Clancy; General Mark W. Clark; Sir Arthur C. Clarke; William Sloan Coffin; President Clinton's Secretary of Defense, William S. Cohen; CIA Director William Colby; Pat Conroy; Walter Cronkite; Michael Crichton; Phyllis Diller; J.P. Donlevy; John Dunning; Jimmy Durante; David Eisenhower; Ambassador John S.D. Eisenhower; Nobel Laureate William Faulkner; The President of Costa Rica, Jose Maria Figueres; Tom Fleming; Betty Friedan; General James M. Gavin; Senator Barry M. Goldwater; Vice President Al Gore; Ambassador Averell Harriman and his wife, Ambassador Pamela Harriman; Helen Hayes; Todd Duncan and Anne Brown, the original "Porgy" and "Bess" in the opera by George Gershwin; Vice President Hubert H. Humphrey; Senator Ted Kennedy; Secretary of State Henry A. Kissinger; Francesce Rhee, the wife of Korean President Syngman Rhee; Senator Henry Cabot Lodge; Robert Ludlam; General of the Army Douglas MacArthur; William Manchester; Judith Martin ("Miss Manners"); David McCullough; Robert S. McNamara; Athos and Sara Menaboni; Lawson Neel; Paul

Newman and Joanne Woodward; Leslie Nielsen; Justice Sandra Day O'Connor; Luciano Pavarotti; Robert and Ida Prosky; Albert A. Riley; Mark Russell; "Green Beret" Staff Sergeant Barry Sadler; Arthur Schlesinger; Michael and Jeff Shaara, Robert Sherrod; Hugh Sidey; Ethel Smith; Hedrick Smith; Alexandre Solzhenitsyn; John Philip Sousa, III; Irving and Jean Stone; Thor Sundt; Strobe Talbott; General Maxwell D. Taylor; Antal Dorati; Mstislav Rostropovich; Edward Teller; John Marks Templeton; Mrs. (Bess) Truman; President Truman's Secretary of the Treasury, John Snyder; Clark Clifford; Margaret Truman; Lucian K. Truscott, IV; Gore Vidal; Mike Wallace; Andy Warhol; Thomas J. Watson, Jr.; General William C. Westmoreland; Bailey White; George F. Will; Garry Wills; Jay Winik; Tom Wolfe; Bob Woodward; and George Zoritch.

Music has played a very important part in my life. Being a pianist and a composer has opened many doors at just the right moment. As one example, I wrote a March and dedicated it to my West Point Class for our 25th Reunion at the Academy in 1977. Our Class was the 150th Class to graduate from the Academy, so the March is entitled "The Sesquicentennial March." The first ensemble to perform this work was the United States Military Academy Band at a parade at West Point. In the reviewing stand at that performance was the Director of the United States Marine Corps Band in Washington, DC, who asked if his Band could perform it in Washington. Later that year, The Marine Band performed it at a summer concert on the steps of the U.S. Capitol. In the audience that evening was Dr. Howard Mitchell, the Director of the

Washington National Symphony, who informed me that, if I would add "strings" to the score and make it into a symphonic piece, the Orchestra would like to play it. After the necessary string parts were added, I, with my wife and three sons, were honored to attend the premier performance in Constitution Hall, the home of the Daughters of the American Revolution in Washington, DC. Through the "musicians' grapevine", Dr. Edgard Doneux, the Director of the Chamber Orchestra of Belgium (R.T.B.), requested permission to include my March in the program for the 1979 Concert in Brussels, Belgium, celebrating the 1,000th Anniversary of the Founding of the City of Brussels in the year 979. At the time of this Concert, I had the honor of serving as the Chairman of the Washington (DC) Chamber Orchestra. Although I personally was unable to attend the performance in Brussels, the Chamber Orchestra went in my place and performed another Concert in that City at that time.

POSTSCRIPT

As I look back over my life, I am reminded daily of the many blessings that God has bestowed on it. He gave me a good family foundation, a great education, a wonderful collection of friends, a loving wife of almost forty-five years, three superb sons, three delightful daughters-in-law, five terrific grandchildren, my continuing good health and a reasonably sane mind. He gave me many talents and told me to use them wisely, but not to take credit for them, for they were a gift from Him. I am very thankful that I have been able to serve my family, my Alma Mater, my Country and my God for these many years; and I sincerely hope that I shall have the opportunity to continue to do so for many years to come.

The Dash

I read of a man who stood to speak
at the funeral of a friend.
He referred to the dates on the tombstone
from the beginning to the end.
He noted that first came the date of his birth
and spoke of the last with tears,
But he said what mattered most of all
was the dash between the years.

It matters not how much we own -
the cars, the house, the cash.
What matters is how we live and love
and how we spend our dash.

So think about this long and hard.
Are there things you'd like to have changed?
You never know what time is left
that can still be re-arranged.

So when your eulogy is being read
with your actions to rehash,
Would you be proud of the things that are said
about how you spent your dash?

Linda Ellis

CPSIA information can be obtained
at www.ICGtesting.com
Printed in the USA
BVOW03*1258311017
499164BV00003B/6/P